THE WINNING MINDSET

Soaring With The Eyes Of An Eagle

By

Sugar Ray Destin, Jr.

Co-authored by Powerful World Changers

2022

The Winning Mindset

Sugar Ray Destin, Jr.
and
Powerful World Changers

First Printing: 2022

ISBN: 979-8-9860894-9-2

Ordering Information:

Special discounts are available on quantity purchases by corporations, associations, educators, and others. For details, contact the publisher at the email listed below.

U.S. trade bookstores and wholesalers:
Please contact info@businessofbooksmastermind.com.

DEDICATION

This book is dedicated to my son, Zayden, my Niecee Makhi, and all the young people chasing their dreams. Live your dreams and always soar beyond the limitations of others!

TABLE OF CONTENTS

FOREWORD

When we were asked to write the foreword for this book, we jumped at the opportunity. The topic of having a winning mindset exemplifies our son and the authors in this book. To give you some context, we have shared a little about the character of our baby boy. We know that you'll enjoy this book as much as we have watched him grow through life and become the man he is today.

Sugar Ray is very much into God. His beliefs are inspiring. As a teenager he became a bible study teacher. He started off as a toddler at a Montessori school. Later he went on to attend St. Christopher Catholic School for his kindergarten year. He was tested to get into public school at the age of 5 for his first-grade year He read his sister's books as early as one years old. He also used to beg his sister to read to him in those early days.

He learned at a high level by paying attention to others while observing their skills. He's very meticulous about his work and passionate about helping others. He's always thought beyond his years. He does not like being around negativity. He often says, "If you can't say anything nice, then don't say it at all."

He's focused on his goals and will not let obstacles stand in his way. He thrives under pressure and carries himself with a spirit of excellence.

Carolyn J. Destin

As a parent, first of all I need to congratulate my son, Sugar Ray, for picking himself back up by his bootstraps. He took time to slowly and strategically planning his work, then working his plan. He should take a serious look in the mirror and pat himself on the back for how far he's come.

Sugar Ray has always been an overachiever. Especially when it comes to educational school programs. He was always able to overcome obstacles because once he put his mind to really learn something, he gave it his all. People think it's easy for him because they're looking from the outside in. However, we've seen the hours of frustration he endures and how hard he works to get to the point that he's risen to.

Sugar Ray Destin, Sr.

PREFACE

To each of you reading this book, we want to thank you. There are many other noteworthy books on the shelf, and you chose to add this book to your collection. We truly appreciate you for making that decision.

Inside the pages of this book, you will read some amazing stories about triumph in the face of adversity. You will be challenged to walk into a new realm of possibilities for your life. The phenomenal authors in this book come from a variety of backgrounds including entrepreneurs, speakers, mental health specialists, brand managers, professional athletes, movie producers, educators, financial planners, and world changers. Each author has shared strategies to help you live your best life and reframe your mental capacity. If you apply the tips given in this book, you will find yourself soaring to a level in your life.

This book was designed to be a complete movement that shifts the dynamic and changes lives around the globe. There is also a workbook and coaching program that compliments this book. Please be sure to grab you copy of the workbook and connect with a certified Winning Mindset Coach to take your life to the highest level possible.

We would love to hear about your future success. From the bottom of our hearts, we love you, believe in you, and are rooting for your ultimate success!

Signed with love,

The Authors of The Winning Mindset

LIST OF AUTHORS IN CHAPTER ORDER

1. Sugar Ray Destin, Jr.
2. Adrienne E. Bell
3. Channell M Dawson
4. Charles Woods
5. Chip Baker
6. Darryl W. Thomas, Jr.
7. Derrick Pearson
8. Deuce Malone
9. Ereka Howard, M.S.
10. Hoss Tabrizi
11. Kenneth Wilson
12. Kristen Davis
13. Monica Earl Washington
14. Reggie Rusk

DESTINED FOR GREATNESS!
Sugar Ray Destin, Jr.

From the earliest stages of my life, I remember having a very competitive spirit. It's something that been instilled in me by my parents and older sister. There are certain values that I learned from them that has kept me moving forward throughout my life. From the outside looking in, people often look at the accomplishments and assume that it was easy. In some cases, it was. In other situations, the accomplishments came with a heavy cost.

As early as fourth grade, I remember competing with my classmates. We had a computer in the back of our math class. Our teacher would let the first two students who completed their work spend the rest of the class period playing a math game on the computer. A few of us began to learn her system. We started working to get ahead and teach ourselves. Every night we would do the problems so that we could be first in turning our work in. It may just seem like kids being proactive, but it was the beginning of much more.

After the first six weeks of fourth grade, we started to realize that this was a circle of competition enroute to being the smartest in the school. We started to compete to see who would have the most 100's on our report cards. We had an exclusive group only open to the five of us. The great thing about our group was that we helped each other and challenged each other to excel academically. Though we came from different backgrounds and ethnicities, we became friends and empowered each other. After elementary we each went on to enroll in magnet schools. Though we lost contact over the years, we kept the same intensity throughout middle and high school. Each of us went on to prestigious colleges across the nation.

I learned a few lessons from the competition we had in fourth grade. I learned the importance of surrounding myself with people who challenged me to be my best self. I learned to look beyond racial barriers. I learned to separate myself from and stay ahead of the crowd. I learned to reward myself for hard work and to handle business before I chased enjoyment. Most importantly, I learned how to think like the teacher and master my craft.

These lessons were learned at such an early age that you would think it was easy to follow the lessons throughout my life. Well, yes and no. The neighborhood I grew up in was not one that rewarded me for being a scholar. It was one that celebrated the accomplishments of athletes, hustlers, and "cool kids". Though I have always been taller than those around me, I didn't fit into these categories.

Let me share a few details about the neighborhood I grew up in. I grew up southeast of the Astrodome in Houston, Texas. The area was not far from William P. Hobby airport and a few things were abundant in the community, including poverty and desperation. At an early age, I learned about the drug culture from an outsider view. There were certain parts of the neighborhood that I was forbidden from frequenting because it contained "bad houses". Those were the houses where drugs were being sold.

The popular older teenagers and young men were the ones who drove fixed up Brougham Cadillacs, Lincoln Town Cars, Buicks, and other models. These cars usually had custom stereo systems, dark tint on the windows, and expensive rims on the tires. We called these cars Slabs and most of the people in the neighborhood looked up to the guys who drove them. These were the fellas who had the money, status, and pretty girls. The other young men in my neighborhood who had status were the athletes or rappers.

Where I grew up, there weren't any professionals to look up to. The only time you heard about a lawyer was if someone caught a charge and was facing jail time. The only doctors in my community had a much lighter hue than my own and were at the local clinic or emergency room. Computers were a luxury and most of us rarely left the six blocks we knew as our 'hood.

I was blessed and cursed though. I grew up with both of my parents who worked decent jobs. They instilled a work ethic that taught me to keep my goals in front of me and always strive to be my best. They taught us that we could have the best in life if we didn't get ate up by our surroundings. They also taught us to remain humble because you never know what life has in store for you. They taught us to keep our friends close and our enemies closer. Though these lessons were simple lessons at face value, you have to add the catalyst of our surroundings into the picture.

I remember going to school and having to apply those lessons daily, especially when I got to middle school and beyond. In middle school everyone was chasing popularity which is normal. The kids at school wore the latest fashion trendy clothing, went to the barber regularly, had Discman's, and even avoided wearing backpacks. You're probably wondering what was significant about wearing a backpack, right? Well, if you wore a backpack, that meant you were probably bringing your work home and got classified as a Nerd. I didn't fit in because of those same reasons. I was studious. I didn't wear name brand clothing. My dad cut my hair. On most days, my backpack was filled with three or four books and the notebooks for my assignments.

I was focused on achieving my goals because I had already seen what life was like outside of those six blocks. My sister is nine years older than me, and she set the tone. She was the athlete in the family and had been heavily recruited as the number one sprinter in the nation. Before my tenth birthday, I had already met some of the top college coaches in the world, multiple Hall of Fame athletes, and had been to a few colleges across the nation for family recruiting visits. My level of exposure exceeded the peer pressure of those around me. That's why my mind has always been set to chasing the next level.

Even though my level of exposure and commitment to achieving my goals was high, the peer pressure was higher. I was what most of the "cool kids" called an easy target for bullying. I didn't respond to the taunts because of my clothing, haircut, or "lack of flavor" unless I absolutely had to. Don't get it twisted, I knew how to fight, I just preferred not to. Again, I've always been taller than my classmates, so I usually had to fight two or more instead of one on one. I was teased a lot for simple things. Looking back at it, those taunts gave me thick skin (I'll explain this later).

While in school, I kept myself active with extracurricular activities. I was in almost everything you could imagine. I played sports, was in J.E.T.S. (Junior Engineering Technological Society), Speech Club, FCA (Fellowship of Christian Athletes), NHS (National Honor Society), and others. I also went to Bible Study at the local church every Tuesday and Wednesday. I guess I enjoyed being around my peers that were focused on going to the next level like I did. When I got to college, I was still active, but I made a lot of silly decisions. I was still involved in leadership on campus but found myself hanging out more than handling my responsibilities. Those poor decisions cost me years of setbacks. I found myself working entry level jobs, because I didn't value the experience and talents I had developed.

One day after work in 2006, I was at my breaking point. I fell to my knees with tears in my eyes and started crying out to God. "God, you've given me all these skills. I've put together conferences, trained half the company I work for, and yet I'm stuck. What am I supposed to be doing because this ain't it?"

I could hear God's voice as clear as day, "Start writing."

I've aways kept whiteboards and notebooks in my house. When I heard that charge, I started writing on one of the whiteboards. The things that were showing up were Motivational Speaker, Youth

Programs, Conferences, Books, Big Crowds, and a few other things. I could even see the small details for the large vision. It was like I was being given my own personal marching orders for success in life. But … I ran!

I was scared of this enormous vision and doubted that I was enough to bring it to fruition. I ran from that vision for almost two years and ducked back into my comfort zone. I put my head back down and worked at the job. I was comfortable there because I still had a consistent paycheck, knew almost everyone in the building and had a set routine. In late 2007, I got out of my own way and started looking at how to make the pieces come together. I started going to Toastmasters to get better as a speaker. I found out very quickly that I had a gift to speak in front of others. My Toastmasters group encouraged me to challenge myself and enroll in competition. I entered the International Speech Contest within 6 weeks of being a member (there's more to the story that I'll share at a different time). The competition has six levels, I advanced to the fourth.

After that, my confidence began to build again, and I started looking for opportunities to speak every chance I could. One Sunday in 2010 while working security at the SXSW International Festival in Austin, I bumped into an old friend from UT. He was passing out his marketing flyers. On the bottom of his flyer were the words Motivational Speaker. I immediately stopped what I was doing and chased him down.

I said, "Bro! Right here on your flyer it says Motivational Speaker. How do I get in?"

He told me that he had an event at JJAEP (Juvenile Justice Alternative Education Program) on Thursday. He would be speaking for an hour so he would give me the last ten minutes. I knew that opportunity waited for no one, so that Thursday I showed up and gave it my best shot. The students and teachers in attendance were blown away. We had a quick conversation after the presentation, and he asked me if I had anything to leave behind for the audience. Long story short I told him I would write a book and have it done in two weeks. Talk about overpromising! That book took me four years to write and changed the direction of my life. While I was writing the book, I was working a decent job while speaking occasionally at local events, schools, colleges, and businesses. I didn't see the need to finish the book because I was already in a good spot financially and was still able to do what I loved as a hobby.

I learned one of the hardest lessons of my life in those four years. While I was at this decent job, I was making good money, but I was miserable because I wasn't chasing my calling. I learned the meaning of the famous quote by Kevin O'Leary, "A salary is just the drug they give you when they want you to give up on your dreams."

As long as I was working at the job, most of my skills and talents were being suppressed. I was missing time with my family, had to ask for permission to go when speaking opportunities arose, and even had to ask for permission to go to the bathroom. Sound familiar?

Finally, I made the decision to leave the company and began to pursue the marching orders I had been given in 2006. I felt so much freedom and quickly began to realize that there is no limit. I started getting more invitations to speak and even started a youth program on July 1, 2014. The funny thing about living your dream is that it will be a combination of the best of times and the worst of times. While I was beginning to flourish, life at home was getting rough financially and my son's mom decided that I would have to chase my dreams alone. What a sacrifice, I was beginning to live my dream but lost my family in the process. I was devastated!

I had no choice but to go all in for my dreams from that day forward. I made up my mind that I would always give everything I had to make my dreams a reality. I published that book, ***Claim Your Destiny***, in July of 2015. When I opened that first box of books, I was sitting across from a seven-year-old young man. He looked at me with this look of pride and said, "Dad, when I get older, I wanna be a speaker and an author too!"

I did all I could to hold the tears back in that moment. Two years later, when he was nine years old, we published his first book, **Zayden's Awesome Adventures**. The following year he went on his first book signing tour. The next year, at the age of eleven, he had his first paid speaking engagement. I then realized that I was building a legacy and his eyes were watching. That fueled me even more.

Let's take a step back and revisit the youth program. That program impacted hundreds of lives in Central Texas. It's been a huge success with a 95% graduation rate. Several of the young men and women went on to college and are doing well for themselves. We were exposing the young men and women to people who came from backgrounds like their own and were doing well in life. We introduced them to Grammy Nominated Musicians, Hall of Fame Athletes, College Professors, Political Activists, Computer Programmers, and many others. We took them on college visits and allowed them to sit in on college classes. We even had a few young authors come out of the program.

Meanwhile, I was still speaking and had my first nationwide book tour. People began to ask me how to write their books and the rest is history. I started a coaching program and eventually launched our publishing company. To date we have launched over 300 Bestselling Authors and 57 International Bestselling Authors.

The goal has always been to perform at my highest level. Like I said before, it has come at a heavy cost. What most people on the outside see is someone who has it all together. The truth is that these accomplishments have been a result of long hours spent working to make the dreams a reality. It has been a sacrifice of time spent away from friends and family. I have had my name drug in the mud by people that I have given my last to help elevate to higher levels.

Through it all, the goal has always been the same … help as many people as I can to achieve their dreams and leave a legacy for the generations coming behind me. That's what a winning mindset is to me, sticking to your principles, empowering others to succeed, and understanding that you're going to ruffle a few feathers along the way.

In the midst of it all, I want to remind you that you were born to win. I challenge you to tap into your personal level of greatness and focus on being the best version of yourself possible. Remember, on the road to your dreams, some people will love you and some will hate you. OWN YOUR LANE AND ... SUCCEED ANYWAY!

ABOUT THE AUTHOR:

See Lead Author's Bio in About the Author section.

THE PRICE IS THE PRICE!
Adrienne E. Bell

Have you ever had a meeting with a potential client that seemed interested in your services? Did the potential client show extreme enthusiasm about working with you based on your rave reviews? After just a few minutes of engaging with you, the prospect bursts with excitement, seemingly ready to close the deal. In your mind, you are thinking, here we go! This sale is going to be easy. Look how excited he is to close the deal? As the client tells you how this was a "divine connection" and they know you are "assigned" to their project, you begin to prepare the invoice because you are SURE they are ready to pay the deposit right on the spot. Then—it happens. The perspective consumer blurts out one of the most cringe-worthy statements in the ears of the entrepreneur, "IS THAT THE PRICE!?"

Or how about this one, "Are you running any specials?"

I love when they say, "Is there any way I can get a discount?"

Here's my favorite, "I was on Google and the services you are offering do not cost that much! People actually pay you that much?"

First of all, the AUDACITY some people have in thinking you should discount your product or service to fit their budget or imagination—is ridiculous! THE PRICE IS THE PRICE! As a Brand Management Expert, I have engaged with countless clients who underestimated the cost of my time, value, and worth to their project. They'd made a gross miscalculation that for me to work with them, I was required to lower my price to accommodate their imagination. It is one thing if I OFFERED a discount on my services, but to DEMAND a discount is absurd. My assignment is to encourage you to STOP allowing people to adjust the price of your products, goods, or services just because they demand it.

It is not your duty to allow new and existing clients to guilt you into lowering your price. Some service providers whose resumes and accomplishments match the price they are charging. For example, I am a 20x Amazon Best Selling Publisher, Film Producer of a movie currently on Amazon Prime, and a Brand Development expert with nearly two decades of accounting and finance experience. If my Executive Brand Development Package is $25,000, I have the knowledge, expertise, resources, and "receipts" to charge what I charge. Respectfully and humbly speaking. Where are your receipts?

It is vital to your success as an entrepreneur to develop your pricing structure based on industry-standard rates AND your receipts. If you are just getting started, you may want to charge a reasonable amount to help build your clientele, assisting you in creating a robust catalog of the services you have provided or sales generated. An expert is anyone who has spent 10,000 hours or more in a specific field. If you have less than 10,000 hours of experience, you must be considerate of potential clients when creating your pricing model. When you don't have the receipts, you must bring the VALUE to your client. For instance, when I was dismissed from my 6-figure corporate job for a Houston energy company in October 2015, I was given a severance package. I took my family to Disney World and launched full-time into my entrepreneurial efforts. When I first started publishing books for others, I only had my first book as an example. I had created an excellent marketing plan, a stellar launch event, and eventually a successful book tour. I put in the work to make myself more marketable and create the receipts adding value to my worth as an entrepreneur. My book, *Becoming an Intentional Wife: A REAL Wife's Guide to Excellence in Marriage and Life*, was a huge success! Even though I only had one book under my belt, my clients realized my VALUE of being a veteran wife to my husband, Donald, since 2000 and my experience as an entrepreneur. I was a product of my product. I was my own client FIRST. Clients realized my VALUE of working in corporate America, so they knew I understood finance, accounting, marketing, and other aspects of a business. I realized my value, but I understood my worth based on my receipts and expertise that potential clients could quickly identify.

What is the difference between value and worth? I'm so glad you asked! Your worth is how people view you. Your value is how you want people to view you. It is your responsibility to communicate how beneficial (valuable) you are to their project. It is up to them to see if the value (benefits) you presented to them is "worth" paying for!

You cannot effectively create and sell your products or services until you GET CLEAR about your worth to the client and value to yourself. You first have to view pricing your products and services from the customer's point of view, NOT YOURS. Then you have to create an incredibly sexy pricing model where they see the value you see and realize you're worth it! Regardless of what you decide your pricing is, at the end of the day, THE PRICE IS THE PRICE!

You do not have to make excuses for charging clients fairly for your services. Gucci, Louis Vuitton, Dior, Chanel, and other luxury brands do not care if you think that handbag or perfume is "worth" what they are charging. In contrast, they value their brand enough to create a product THEY would buy. Would YOU pay the price you are charging clients? If the price is the price, make sure it is a price YOU would actually pay. Even though I have clients who compensate me upwards of $25,000 to develop their brands, I have paid double that amount to have certain aspects of my business serviced by vendors. In other words, I will never charge what I am unwilling to pay. I value my services, expertise, and receipts enough to know I can charge what I charge because I would pay what I charge. Would you pay your price?

There is an epidemic in entrepreneurship where service providers are not only OVERCHARGING clients, but most are UNDERCHARGING. If you struggle knowing your value to yourself and your worth to the client, don't beat yourself up. We have all been there.

People say, "Know your worth," but the saying needs to be amended to "Know your value so others will understand your worth."

I want to encourage you to ask yourself, "Do I know my worth to potential clients, and am I valuing myself properly?"

Here are a few tips to a WINNING MINDSET when it comes to pricing structure:

1. The price is the price. Period. Do not allow anyone to cause you to change your price.

2. If you decide to change your price or discount your services, let it be YOUR decision. Do not be coerced into lowering your standards OR your price. If you wouldn't do it, don't do it for the client.

3. Be fair to the client as well as yourself. Whether you have 10,000 hours of experience or ten, you are valuable and your worth is NEVER for sale.

4. The days of the "solopreneur" are over. People treat you differently when they think you are operating alone. They take their entitlement to lower prices to another level when they feel you are the only one pocketing the profit. To scale your business to a six, seven, or eight-figure business, you must build a team and a system that can be automated. You have the potential to deliver high-quality services to your clients and reach greater earning potential when you create the right system and build the right team. Having a team and an automated business model will automatically justify your pricing model. or your business. I made the mistake of thinking I could do it alone. While gifted as an award-winning publisher, film producer, and brand executive, I realized I would only earn at the level I could

execute. I would often bite off more than I could chew to justify my "worth." The moment I built a system and a team, my net profit increased immediately.

5. Price your goods and services to actually turn a profit. Make sure you price your services where you net between 40-50% of your gross revenue. That is an aggressive number, but it is a good goal to reach for as you are creating or revamping your pricing structure. If you can't keep it between 40-50, do your best not to go below 20%.

6. Be humble but confident when establishing your prices. Don't allow fear of losing the sale to keep you from being paid fairly. Don't allow yourself to compare your pricing structure to another service provider. Remember, they may have skills, expertise, or experience that you may not have. On the contrary, you may need to increase your price if you have training or experience that someone else may not have.

7. The more you grow as a service provider, the more you should charge. With the cost of inflation, gas prices, and the cost of goods, you must find out how much you are spending on supplies to ensure you are making a profit. If you are in the creative business, such as myself, make sure you create a pricing structure that does not have you making less than the federal minimum wage. For example, one of my clients is an illustrator. It takes her about forty hours to create a thirty-two-page children's book. Before working with her, she was only charging $250 per book. That means if it took her forty hours to illustrate a children's book at $250.00 per book, she was only making $6.25 per hour. That is less than the federal minimum wage of $7.25! I had to walk her through changing her entire pricing structure to match the quality of work she was creating AND the time it took her to make it. To add insult to injury, that forty hours did NOT include revisions. Sometimes she was making less than $4.00 an hour, depending on how long the revisions took and the number of revisions. The price is the price, but for some of us, the price is NOT RIGHT!

Ask yourself these questions:
1. How much is my hour worth?
2. Who is my ideal client and why?
3. What are my deal-breakers when securing a client?
4. Where can I find my ideal client?
5. Why am I struggling with properly pricing my products and services? Fear? Shame? Value? Worth?

My fellow entrepreneur do not be afraid to alter your price to match your value. Be vigilant as you count up the cost of the TIME it takes to service your client. How much is your hour worth? I currently charge $265.00 per hour or $750.00 for three hours for my Signature Brand Think Tank, but you better believe that I am charging what I am worth and ensuring my client sees the value in my expertise. I learned a valuable lesson the hard way; if they cannot pay my invoice, they are not my client. Plain and simple. I only attract those who are looking for me. Who are you attracting? Are you attracting people with a poverty mindset? Are you attracting people who look for discounts and rebates versus value and quality? Do you do to vendors what you don't want clients to do to you? In other words, do you ask for discounts and rebates? You cannot become upset with clients when they ask for deals if you do the same thing to other service providers. You reap what you sow.

'You get what you pay for,' is not just a cliché. When my clients pay my fees, they get more than what my package is "worth" in the "value" I bring to the table. Are you having trouble with pricing? Hire a brand strategist or pricing specialist to help you create or reconfigure your pricing model. You cannot grow your business effectively until you know how to charge the right price for the service you are providing. The price is the price! Don't discount yourself and don't let anyone else do it either!

ABOUT THE AUTHOR:

Social Media:
IG @therealadriennebell
FB @therealadriennebell
LinkedIn: @adrienneebell
Email therealadriennebell@gmail.com

Adrienne E. Bell is a 22x Amazon Bestselling Publisher, Executive Producer of the soul-stirring Amazon Prime movie, "When the Soul Cries: Trauma. Tears. Triumph." and Executive Brand Management Expert.

"My superpower is to energize, empower, and encourage executives, authors, coaches, speakers, and thought leaders to be legendary in business, love, and relationships. Let's Work!"

SIGNATURE TALKS

1. **The Price Is The Price!** - *"The price is the price, but for some of us, the price is NOT RIGHT!"*
2. **The Wifeabilty Framework** - *"If you don't friend well, you won't wife well."*
3. **Loyalty Is Optional** - *"Don't expect loyalty from others when you aren't loyal to yourself."*

SERVICES OFFERED

- *Brand Development*
- *Brand Management*
- *Project Management*
- *Non-Profit Development*
- *Revenue Planning*
- *Event Planning & Management*
- *Product Development & Launches*
- *Website Development and SEO*
- *Business Funding & More!*

A BETTER LIFE
Channell M. Dawson

In the beginning, God created...those are the five most powerful words in the Bible. When God finished working on Creation, He saw that it was good. Not only was it good, but it was also created perfectly. In God's master plan, He gave specific instructions for His creation's design. Now, since we are writing about the winning mindset let's look at the word created.

The Word Created

The word created, by its main definition—is causing something to happen because of one's actions. Another definition of the word created is to bring something into existence. But this definition is unique; it says the word created is to originate by playing a character for the first time. Now, we just said that the five most powerful words in the Bible were, "In the beginning God created!" God's character, in the beginning, sought to bring His righteousness into natural existence through the creation of mankind spiritually first (Genesis 1:27) and then naturally (Genesis 2).

To obtain a winning mindset, one must have the mind of Christ. 1 Corinthians 2:10-15 says, "God's Spirit has shown you everything. His Spirit finds out everything, even what is deep in the mind of God" (CEV). But God has given His spirit. Therefore, we don't think the same way that people of the world think. This is also why we can recognize the blessings God has given us.

Your Words Have POWER!

Every word we speak comes to us by God's spirit, not by human wisdom. And this same Spirit helps us teach spiritual things to spiritual people. Therefore, only someone who has God's Spirit can understand spiritual blessings. Anyone who does not have God's Spirit thinks these blessings are foolish. People guided by the Spirit can make all kinds of judgments, but they cannot be subject to the judgments of others.

A winning mindset directed by the Spirit of God is a mindset funded by heaven. A Christ-centered family is a danger to the works of the adversary and his army. This is what we were created for to win, mind, body, and soul. More importantly, a winning mindset creates other winning mindsets. This is the foundation of leadership and the domino effect to create greater leaders.

When we talk about mindset, we are talking about the results of our inner thoughts made manifest in our day-to-day interactions and dealings with other human beings.

My grandmother used to say, "treat people how you want to be treated and you'll never be mistreated."

Now, in some aspects, this has been very true. But in others, it is not because you could be the nicest person to the rudest people, and they'll take your kindness for weakness.

On the other hand, you could be rude to the nicest people and miss out on an opportunity to make new friends. Having a winning mindset strengthened by the instructions of the Holy Spirit is a jackpot mindset. Everyone wants to win the Powerball Jackpot but it's the ones that don't play that hold the winning numbers. Now, say that out loud slowly!

If we don't apply what is in us, we will never strike it rich mentally, spiritually, emotionally, or financially. We must apply wisdom to achieve a winning mindset. If we've never done a specific thing before such as skating or bowling, we can't speak about the impact it would have on another person. The truth is our experience produces a winning mindset in those who we oversee. That's our children, spouse, siblings, and even our parents.

The fact is no one practices losing but everyone trains to win!!!

Remember these tips:

1. We were created by God in His image and His likeness and just like He is—we are perfect!

2. Winning is what we were created to do!

3. Our mind is designed to win!!!

4. When we set our mind on things greater than our current situations winning is our portion!!!

5. Nothing or no one can stop a winning mindset because it is focused on the finish line, not the audience or onlookers!!!

Developing a Winning Mindset

Winners know that on their way to the finish line there will be times that they may slip, stumble, and even fall but their get-up will be better than their take-off. Winners don't focus on the fans they focus on the finish line. Winners know that when they get to the finish line of their current level that it's time to start training for their next level.

A winning mindset is constantly conditioned to master the tasks ahead, whether it is at work, home, church, community, or just grocery shopping. This winning mindset will prepare you to finish strong and with great wisdom. Winners seek wisdom before venturing into uncharted territories which is a necessary part of becoming wise in their overall life.

So how do we discover and develop a winning mindset? I'm glad you asked! The first evidence that you are developing a winning mindset is when you realize that the mindset you have been operating in is causing you to go backward instead of forward. The dog going back to its own vomit syndrome! The Bible says in Proverbs 26:11 "As a dog returns to his vomit, so is a fool who repeats his folly" (NHEB). Who wants to keep repeating the same cycles over and over?

Most would say that, but the truth is that many have fallen for this practice from generation to generation. Another truth about discovering a winning mindset is to reject the negativity of others concerning what you can and cannot do or what you are and are not capable of. Negative thoughts, feelings, and people will cause us to prematurely give birth to our gift or talent before it is fully developed.

Now that we've mentioned developing our gifts let's touch on it. According to the *Oxford English Dictionary,* the definition of the word develop is "grow or cause to grow and become more mature, advanced, or elaborate." Developing a winning mindset takes time and dedication. Sometimes we lose friends and family when our mindset shifts from barely making it to winning. At this point, we must condition our hearts to release anything and anyone that will cause us to withdraw our rights to achieve what we've been working towards. The truth is that we were created to win! Anything that stands in the way of our success we should be willing to lay it aside until we achieve what we desire in our heart to achieve.

Whether it's a stronger marriage, a deeper relationship with God, a higher paying job, a higher degree in education, or just more stability in life it is ours to achieve; and if we fail, we can't blame our parents or our peers because the truth is—our destiny is our responsibility after we take that step into adulthood. You see, in our youth, our parents are examples of what our next season should look like. If it turns out that our parents are not good examples, we must find someone that we can see ourselves resembling in the future.

Now, some people look at celebrities, athletes, or even businessmen/women as examples of what they desire their future to look like. Whatever method is used—it should always assist us with gaining momentum when trying to achieve a winning mindset. Most would think that developing a winning mindset is easy, but I am here to tell you that you will have to work hard to achieve a winning mindset and you will have to work harder to keep it! So, you see developing a winning mindset is hard work and it makes us a target when we achieve it.

There is a person assigned to every one of us to assist us with developing into a greater version of ourselves which contributes to us getting to our next level. Now, some people will delay their mindset from being elevated from a mediocre mindset to a winning mindset because they cannot connect with the person that holds the key to their next promotion. This person can be their parents, mature peers, mature coworkers, lead manager, executive manager, or just a stranger on the streets. Yes, I said a stranger on the street because the Bible says in Hebrews 13: 2, that we should not forget to entertain strangers because we could be entertaining angels without knowing (paraphrased). I know what you are saying, entertain strangers in the condition of the world today? Yes! Yes! Yes! A winning mindset is focused on the connection, then communication, and finally the completion of the assignment. Once the assignment is complete the purpose and prosperity will explode and overflow into something that will bless one generation to the next. Yes, a winning mindset is focused on developing generational wealth!

Finally, we've reached the final stretch in the chapter. Now, since we mentioned generational wealth let's talk about it. Back in our grandparent's generation they were not afforded the opportunities we have today, yet they had a winning mindset. They never complained about not having this or that; they just went out and found ways to make ends meet. Generational wealth is not as important today as it was back then. Our grandparents had land, houses, and businesses that should have been passed down from one generation to the next but somewhere along the way, a losing mindset overtook the one who should have been transferring the wealth to the next generation. Therefore, a winning mindset transfer must take place before anything significant is passed down from one generation to the next. Yes, a winning mindset can be transferred; it's called training!

Training For a Winning Mindset

Training is very important to maintain a winning mindset and secure generational wealth. This training starts in our childhood. The Bible says in Proverbs 22:6 that we should train up our children in the way they should go so that when they are older and wiser, they will not depart from what we have instilled in them when they were younger (paraphrased). Generational wealth is not just money, it's recipes from our grandmother, it's a collection of antiques that have been well preserved from one generation to the next, it's a car that has been cared for to give as a graduation gift from one generation to the next. It can be something as simple as a pair of pearl earrings that were worn by our great-grandmother on her wedding day. We should be concerned with passing down these legacies to the next generation because eventually, they will hold so much inherent value with the power to restore a generation in its time of need. Never doubt the latent power within these legacies!

A willing mindset is concerned about the condition of the family lineage and how to preserve what our ancestors worked so hard to obtain. We must continue to assist those family members around us to gain a winning mindset so that we can carry out the purpose and plan for the lineage of our heritage. Some traditional things made our ancestors strive in business and overall life such as family reunions, cookouts, and family vacations in the summer. Everyone has had that one cousin with the winning mindset to plan each event and budget it down to the penny just so the family would have a good time and not break the bank! Now, that's the cousin that everyone respected. That was the cousin with the winning mindset and a mansion! That's the cousin that everyone was intimidated by but that's also the cousin that would give you the shirt off their back and the last dollar from his or her pocket.

Bring It All Together: Developing the Character of a Winner

In closing, to maintain a winning mindset we must develop the character of a winner. Winners never focus on someone else's winnings; they develop a plan and strategy that will put them on a fast track to their own success. The old saying "winners never cheat and cheaters never win" is a true statement because a winning mindset is constantly exchanging one lever for the next. A winning mindset is on to the next level before they even get comfortable in their current level. A winning mindset is in constant battle with itself and has very little time to compete with others. A winning mindset is working on overachieving so that there is very little possibility of not achieving their goals.

If we don't try new adventures, there are amazing life experiences that will pass us by! A winning mindset is equivalent to a credit card with no limit. There is no limit to where a winning mindset will take the one who is operating within it. There are so many ways to win in the world today and many will never experience any of them because their mindset is stuck on surviving and not winning. We must reprogram our minds to win and not just survive because as human beings those faculties are innate—the necessities to survive—but dominion to win and rule over everything on the earth is ours for the taking! The exception to this rule is that we want to rule over each other and allow the things we have dominion over to rule us. Is that backward or what?!

The key to maintaining and mastering a winning mindset is the remember who you are and *Whose* you are when it's time to level up. Never dumb down, never exaggerate and never ever allow anyone to make you abort your purpose because they can't handle your shine. Keep an extra pair of shades and keep shining bright for all to see because you were born to win!

ABOUT THE AUTHOR:

Social Media:
IG @cdawson0425
FB @cdawson0425
LinkedIn: @channelldawson
Email cdawson0425@gmail.com

Mrs. Channell Maiden Dawson, serves as an employee of the federal government for sixteen years, including positions in leadership. She enjoys using these leadership skills to develop other leaders.

Dawson draws inspiration from her husband of 18 years, 15-year-old daughter, and her three-year-old boy/girl twins. In Mrs. Dawson's free time, activities include motivational speaking, encouraging leaders to be greater leaders, working with underprivileged individuals with avenues to become privileged in their endeavors, and undereducated individuals to seek means of higher education for career and life advancement.

Dawson earned an Associate's Degree in Christian Counseling along with 19 years of experience in marriage, parenting, and career counseling. She holds multiple life coaching certifications including master life coach, life purpose coach, happiness life coach, mindset coach, cognitive behavior coach, goal success coach, and professional life coach.

Channell M. Dawson serves as the President of Lifestyle Restoration Group (LRG) a 501c3 non-profit organization that provides an opportunity for growth and development in whatever portion of our client's life that seems to be unfruitful or unproductive whether is a failing marriage, broken relationship, or lack of motivation in you career path we can help get our clients to get back on the road to success.

At the end of every encounter with individuals or family units, her mission is to assist them with the pursuit of living a blessed life so everyone can see them live their best lives and prove the doubters wrong.

THINK GREAT DO GREAT BE GREAT
Charles Woods

Life is about choices, making the best choice for your well-being, and the well-being of those in your presence. Life is not always good but there are opportunities every day, every hour, every minute, every second to change your outcomes, but only if that is your desire.

I would get up early on Saturday mornings and was excited to be able to watch cartoons if the antennas on our television worked properly. It was not a big deal if the antennas did not work, I could still watch a movie using the family VCR. The excitement that early Saturday morning was not really about the cartoons or the movie. The excitement came from having the electricity on after not having electricity for a few weeks. That was kind of the routine. Having the opportunity to watch local television channels or a movie, lighting up a room, or listening to music was not taken for granted. These privileges were small to a lot of my peers but a big deal for me. I was grateful for these types of opportunities and very optimistic that they would last.

Being grateful starts with not complaining about doing without or experiencing an undesirable situation. Being grateful is about appropriating all that you have and taking a positive outlook even when times are hard. Things could be worse. Spending time being envious of what other people have, comparing situations, or wishing things were better with no actions will send you into a state of misery. The key is to develop a plan that is focused on having a better life and implementing that plan. You control your future and everything in it.

Trait: Grateful

- For every day you get to open your eyes and have an opportunity to be better
- For the individuals that came before you and made it possible for you to have these opportunities
- For everyone that took the time to support you on your journey

I was lifting weights and running at the high school athletic facility getting ready for the high school football season. Not a care in the world while in the weight room bonding with my teammates and getting better.

One of my teammates was just getting off work and as he entered the weight room he asked, "Does anyone want a job this summer? It's outside in the heat and we work ten-hour days with time and a half on Fridays." That was pretty good money for a high school student during the summertime.

Without hesitation I replied, "I do."

Little did my teammate know that this made my day. This was the opportunity I needed. I had recently moved out of my parents' house and was living with one of my friends. The thought of taking care of myself had been weighing on me. I needed some form of income to pay for my essential items and I did not want to be a burden to anyone. I wanted to pay for my own necessities. This job was a great opportunity for me to get over the hump. I never wear my concerns on my face or shoulders. No one knew that I had these concerns, but I was and always will think of ways to make my situation better. Being optimistic and resilient, I knew I would make it through this difficult time. Giving up or making excuses has never and will never be in my DNA. I decided to take advantage of the opportunity that was placed in front of me.

That opportunity made my situation a little easier to deal with. It showed me that no matter what you are facing, there is always an answer. There will always be opportunities that will present themselves. Acceptance of those opportunities is where the decision needs to be made. Understand that these opportunities may not come easy. Decide how bad is the want or need for change. Is the will strong enough to overcome the obstacles? Nothing in life is given, so how are you going to respond?

Trait: Resilient

- Never let your trials and tribulations stop you from accomplishing your goals and improving your situation
- Keep pushing to be the best vision of yourself

I was sitting on the gym floor of the Bernard G. Johnson Coliseum at Sam Houston State University (about forty-five minutes from my high school) waiting patiently for my row to be acknowledged and my name to be called. My last name starts with a "W", so I am toward the end of the program. I looked up in the stands ... to my surprise I saw my mother and father. My eyes connected with the section where they were taking a seat. This was already an exciting time and seeing them made this event a little more special. My parents and I did not have a sit-down discussion about graduation. There were no plans for a senior trip. There were no plans for a graduation party. We did not discuss college or how I was going to get to my college campus on the day I was scheduled to report. We did not communicate much at all.

How many times have we heard the phrase, control what you can control? I concluded as an adolescent that I could only control myself. I love my parents but at that time they were not in a good place to support me and that was okay. They gave me life and I have always been grateful for that. I focused on the uplifting and loving conversations with my mother and cherished the time that my father and I spent together. Those are the things that I chose to focus on. My energy is important, and I will always focus on the positives. Negativity and hate typically gets the most attention in our society and I did not want that to define me. I did not want that to be a part of my journey.

When your body is dragging, and you cannot get up in the morning. When there is an issue with anything and everything. When you continually complain, and the people close to you suddenly are not available. Check your energy, the issue might be you. Energy is important and everyone has the choice of which type of energy will be allowed in and what type of energy will be put out. Life is so much easier when energy is focused in a positive direction.

Trait: Energy

- Your energy controls your productivity
- Your energy will determine your outcomes
- Positive energy and thoughts will drive your success and keep you motivated throughout the process

The alarm sounded and with one eye I looked at the clock. It was 7:15 am. Time to get up. I had an 8:00 am class. As I went through my morning routine, I noticed the two gentlemen that shared a room with me were not moving. I attempted to get them going, but they made the choice to stay in bed. Professors and class time would not wait for anyone, and it was time for me to be on my way.

It's no one's responsibility but mine to ensure that I am always where I need to be and taking care of my business. Being accountable is hard and it is easy to start making excuses or putting the blame for mishaps on someone else.

Each semester I would see inspiring college students come and go. Most of their stories were similar, poor time management. The way they spent their time did not meet the needs of their academic journey.

Time cannot be spent sleeping, playing video games, hanging out with friends, or going to parties. To be a successful student there needs to be some sort of dedication or willingness to develop the skills that will support the journey. If there is no dedication to these types of opportunities, then why spend money to attend a college or university? Why accept a scholarship when there are so few available scholarships and so many individuals willing to put in the hard work to obtain one?

Number one, be accountable for the future success that lies ahead. There are always consequences when work ethic is lacking, and expectations are not followed. Successful teams are successful because every member is accountable for themselves. They effectively and efficiently do their part. No one has to be micromanaged to ensure that they are focused and completing their task. Those teams are filled with individuals that do not want to let their team members down or they are self-motivated. All teams have accountability checks to make sure that the team is on schedule and to sort out any issues or possible issues. The experienced leaders embed the accountability checks within their weekly operations. Team members are more likely to complete their task and hold each other accountable because everyone understands the organization's system. These types of systems will create a strong, positive culture, and an organization that will thrive. Make sure that ANYONE joining the team from outside of the direct organization understands the culture, so the culture is not disrupted.

Trait: Accountable

- There is no individual that can hold you more accountable than yourself. Take on the challenge and monitor yourself
- Be willing to allow someone to take on the responsibility of being your accountability partner when needed

The environment is calm as staff members start arriving on campus. Faces begin to light up and smiles start to emerge as I say good morning. Some staff only need to hear good morning, others would like a professional hug with their good morning. Of course, there are casual conversations here and there, but most of all there is a feeling of positive energy and love in the environment. Professional relationships grow stronger with each day as well as their trust in me as a leader.

"Can I speak with you? I have a concern."

"Do you have a minute; I need your advice?"

"Are you available, I just need to vent?"

These are examples of comments that I receive. They value my response and know I have their best interest in mind. They know that I will be impartial and fair. In this mutually respectful environment, I have gained their trust.

GREAT leaders will take the time to establish trust from the individuals in their organization. Most individuals must know that their leader genuinely cares about them and the organization or it will be very hard to establish trust. GREAT leaders also learn to develop mutual trust for the individuals that they serve. No organization can successfully function with one person doing everything. *So, when you GREAT leaders are gaining the trust of the individuals in your organization, please take the time to genuinely grow your trust in these individuals.*

There are always goals that have been set and work to be done, how these demands are met is a choice. Will there be a positive environment established with motivation and growth? Will there be an environment that has low morale and huge turnover?

Leaders cannot control everything but what they can control is their culture. Remember that leaders are not only the individuals that stand in front of the organization or team. Everyone in the organization or team can be considered a leader, if they are doing their part.

Trait: Trust

- Make sure you are exhibiting characteristics and actions that will build a foundation of trust. Be willing and execute the ability to believe and rely on others
- Always be firm but fair. Lead with a kind heart and care for others, but the expectations are the expectations.

Each of the sections above focused on one of the following traits: Grateful, Resilient, Energy, Accountable & Trust. In those paragraphs there was a life example and a brief description from my point of view. When all five of these traits are put together, they become very powerful and describe what being GREAT really means. These traits have assisted me through my struggles in life and I hope that they can do the same for others.

Use these traits to reflect on how you function in your everyday life and routines. See where you are with being GREAT and adjust when you feel yourself not moving in a GREAT direction. Your loved ones and the people that you serve deserve the best version of you. Everyone should be reflecting daily so there is at least one percent growth from the previous day … learning never stops. When you decide to be GREAT there will be no limits to what you can accomplish. No matter the situation you have a choice. It is your duty to make the best of every opportunity that is placed in front of you. Go Be GREAT!!!

Think GREAT, Do GREAT, Be GREAT

1. Think GREAT (Think of your needs personally and/or professionally and how these traits will support you on your journey of growth.)
   i. How will the five traits support your needs?
2. Do GREAT (Develop a plan that consists of these traits and is focused on your growth. You may have already established one or more of the traits but remember there is always room to grow.)

     i.   What are your plans for implementing these five traits?

3. Be GREAT (This is a lifetime journey that is filled with reflection and adjustments. Continue to put in the work and the outcomes will be GREAT.)

     i.   How will you continue to focus on the five traits to ensure a GREAT Mindset?

ABOUT THE AUTHOR:

Social Media:

IG @charleswoodsww
FB @charleswoodsww
LinkedIn: @charleswoodsww
Email ullgrad1911@hotmail.com

Charles has nineteen years in public education, nine years as a classroom teacher and football coach, six years as a head boys track coach, five years as an assistant principal and this year makes his fifth year as a building principal.

Charles has a M.S. in Engineering and Technology Management and a B.S. in Industrial Technology from the University of Louisiana at Lafayette. He is a four time best selling author for his collaborative work in Black Men Love and The Impact Of Influence Volume 1, 2 and 4. Charles takes pride in being a Positive Mindset and Motivational Mentor, Coach and Speaker. He is married to his beautiful wife Celena Woods and has two daughters Courtney and Chelsea Greer.

His certifications include:
- EC-12 Superintendent Certification
- EC-12 Principal Certification
- EC-12 Special Education Certification
- Rice University Leadership Partner's Executive Education Academy
- Non-Crisis Intervention Trainer

"There is no other profession that gives me the opportunity to impact lives like public education. I did not choose this path; this path chose me. I will continue to be a servant leader to those in my care and for those that choose to work with me. I am forever grateful for this opportunity to make a difference in the lives of our young scholars."

"Don't be a product of your environment, make your environment be a product of the positive you!!!"

MINDSET IS DEVELOPED BY UNDERSTANDING LIMITS, POSSIBILITIES AND OPPORTUNITIES
Chip Baker

A winning mindset, like anything, must be developed. In order to win on a consistent basis, one must have a mindset that continues to grow. A person that understands that there are no limits to what they can achieve, will soar to high heights. A person that understands that great things are possible if they believe and put in the work to make it happen will see that anything can be accomplished. A person that understands that each opportunity sets them up for a bigger opportunity will have opportunities galore.

Limits

"If you limit yourself, you limit yourself."
-Chip Baker

Growing up and until this day I have always been a quiet and reflective guy. The reflection time I have had has allowed me to evaluate the things I do well with but also allows me to evaluate the things I need to be better on. Once I understood the things I needed to be better on I would work on my self-talk to ensure that I am pushing to be the best version of myself. I did not tell anybody, I just did the work and let the results speak for themselves. I would say phrases to myself like "Up your game!", "Push yourself!" and the last few years of my life I have said, "Go get it!" This process has allowed me to learn, by trial and error and experience, that there is no limit to what one can push themselves to achieve. I am the research and the evidence of that.

I never told myself that I could not do anything because as the older generation would say, "Can't never could!" It was a simple thing. Believe and then go achieve. If we think we can't, we can't. If we think we can then we will. Even if we do not reach the desired accomplishment, we will be better for putting in the effort to try. Slow-motion beats no motion any day.

Who is the only person that holds us back from achieving anything we want to achieve in life? Yes, ourselves! There is no limit to what we can achieve. That is the mindset we must grow to have. When we believe that greatness can happen for and to us, it is electrifying. It sets us on a path and gives us the momentum we need to get wherever we want to get in life. If you limit yourself, you limit yourself!

Possibilities

"The possibilities are possible."
-Chip Baker

Many times, we discount ourselves because we feel that maybe we are not good enough or because I do not know anyone that has achieved this or that, I am not capable. I am here to tell you that the possibilities are possible. I was blessed with the opportunity to play college football. Upon my arrival there I realized very quickly that the talent level WAS NOT the same as in high school. There were some phenomenal athletes there. The environment had guys that have achieved huge milestones and awards. As I got around them and observed the scene—I saw that they had next-level things going on. Things that I had never seen done before. They were all bigger, faster, stronger, and meaner! Seeing that created a hunger within me. I realized that there were two options in college because everybody there was good. I could either go home or get better. Going home was really not an option though. As I put my head down and worked, I realized that I too was capable of doing next-level things. I saw that the possibilities were possible.

We make it possible to achieve the things we want to achieve when we believe! We must have the proper mindset by believing that the possibilities are possible for us.

Opportunities

"Opportunities bring opportunities."
-Chip Baker

Opportunities come in all shapes and sizes. Sometimes they may come to us disguised as hard work or by people that we had no idea we have similar things in common. We have to remember that opportunities bring opportunities. I would like to share a personal story to illustrate the importance of being on point with each opportunity we have.

I am a person that believes in having core values that I hold firm to. I was taught this by my family and teams that I have been a part of. I believe in doing right, treating people right, working hard, and surrounding myself with good people. A little over six years ago I started my YouTube channel and podcast, Chip Baker- The Success Chronicles. I realized that I was blessed and fortunate to be around some amazing people. I also had the privilege of having great conversations with them that would be very beneficial in my growth towards success. I decided that I could not keep the valuable information to myself. Those people needed to be highlighted and the valuable knowledge they had needed sharing. I started the YouTube channel and podcast to highlight them. Little did I know that along the journey I would come across more amazing people and learn lots more. I also did not know that I would be getting opportunities to connect, be referred to, get speaking opportunities and eventually become a multiple-time best-selling author.

About three years ago I connected with a couple of men from an amazing men's group. They did a lot of pouring into men all over the country. Eventually, I was asked to speak at one of their virtual events to share my journey and experience. From that opportunity, I connected with and interviewed several of the men that were a part of that group. We have established quality relationships and always support each other's movements. One of the men does book publishing and teaches authors the business of books. That guy connected with me, and we have worked on several projects that have become Amazon #1 bestsellers. That same guy is the visionary for this book that I am writing this chapter for, Sugar Ray Destin Jr. I am forever grateful for the opportunity to live, learn and grow through that process.

Opportunities bring Opportunities! We must be present in each moment with every opportunity we have because we will receive more opportunities down the road. Those opportunities will be based on our ability to be in the moment and be the best version of ourselves with each opportunity we are blessed to have.

"Valuing adds value."
-Chip Baker

We also must remember that each opportunity has value. When we are thankful for what we are blessed to have it shows that we do not take each opportunity for granted. We show that we understand that things could be better, but they could also be much worse. We will gain more opportunities from valuing each experience.

"Choose to have the proper mindset when working on growth."
-Chip Baker

Every choice we make is a life-or-death decision. Each choice can bring us life or cause us to have death based on the mindset in which we view what we are doing. That is why it is important to be in control of our thoughts, our perspectives, and our actions. Our time is valuable and we only get this moment, one time in our life. Have you ever thought about that? Once this moment is over there is no going back.

Strive to be mentally tough. It is tough to get through tough things. The tough things make you tough. Tough people do tough things. Be Mentally Tough! It's a great path!

We become mentally tough by understanding three things. The first is if you limit yourself, you limit yourself. Second, the possibilities are possible. Third, opportunities bring opportunities. Mindset is developed by understanding limits, possibilities, and opportunities.

God bless you on your journey in developing your mindset the right way! Go get it!

ABOUT THE AUTHOR:

Social Media:
IG @chipbakertsc
FB @chipbakertsc
LinkedIn: @chipbakerthesuccesschronicles
Email chipbakertsc@gmail.com

Chip Baker is a fourth-generation educator. He has been a teacher/coach for over twenty-three years. He is a multiple-time best-selling Author, Youtuber/Podcaster, Motivational Speaker and Life Coach.

Chip Baker is the creator of the YouTube channel/podcast "Chip Baker - The Success Chronicles" where he interviews people from all walks of life and shares their stories for positive inspiration and motivation.

Live. Learn. Serve. Inspire. Go get it!

Chip Baker Books

Growing Through Your Go Through
Effective Conversation to Ignite Relationships
Suited For Success Vol. 2
The Formula Chart for Life
The Impact of Influence
R.O.C.K. Solid
The Impact of Influence Vol. 2
Kids Book- Stay On The Right P.A.T.H.
The Impact of Influence Vol. 3
Black Men Love
The Impact of Influence Vol. 4

EYES ON THE HEART
Darryl W. Thomas, Jr.

WHAT DID I GET MYSELF INTO?

You had to see it. To me, it wasn't just a question that was meant to stump me. It was a life decision that I had been presented with. One that would either challenge me to rise above or convince me to cower down and blend in with the crowd.

At that time in my life, I was dating this extraordinary young lady by the name of Alexia Ferguson. She was everything that I could ask for in a woman. It was her outward beauty! It was her attractive figure! It was her intellect! It was her southern draw! It was her maturity and nurturing ways! Oh … and she could cook too!

We met our junior year in high school. In less than a year, we agreed that it was something special about our relationship. So much so that I mustered up the courage to approach her father. Mind you, her dad was old school. No boy or young man was good enough for his little princess. Of course, he had no problem letting you know that you were not the one for his daughter.

He often tried to shoo me away from his property when I would walk Alexia home from school. But like a stray cat that you feed once, I kept coming back again and again. One day, the time came when I made a bold decision to put my life on the line. I had to risk the biscuit – as they say.

I went up to Mr. Ferguson's front porch. I knocked on the door. To my surprise, I was invited inside. As I walked through the living room in search of the room that Mr. Ferguson was in, I scurried to gather my composure. I frantically sought ways to calmly collect my nerves and to reel my heart back inside my chest.

Needless-to-say, I understood the assignment. For me, it was either now or never – in my mind.

I needed to stand ten toes flat and express to this man my true feelings for his daughter. After all, it was my promise to Alexia. Little did her father know, her and I shared a secret that he knew nothing about – she was pregnant with my child. Mind you, had he found out prematurely, I would not be alive to share this life hack to winning with you.

Now… It's one thing to talk about it. Taking a stand for one another and defending our love at all costs is something that Alexia and I talked about often. But it is entirely different when you are challenged and presented with the opportunity to walk it like you talk it.

This was that opportunity for me. I knew it and I refused to blow it.

With nerves checked my heartbeat somewhat under control and a little vibrato in my voice, I looked Old School in the eyes and said, "Mr. Ferguson" as I gulped, "Um… I love your daughter and I want to be with her for a long time. I want to marry her."

The look that followed seemed as if he had momentarily peered into my soul. He was perplexed. Not sure if I was crazy, stupid, or just that bold. I believe that day he detected a little of both.

With calculated moves, Mr. Ferguson looked away. Then he proceeded with a moment of silence.

At that point, I wondered, "What… did I get myself into?"

ARE YOU SURE?

I didn't know if he was going to go slap crazy on me or start shooting. Regardless, I was prepared to bob and weave if needed, or to even duck and cover. But what I was *NOT* going to do was back down from what I believed in.

I believed in us. I believed in the love that Alexia and I shared. I believed in the possibilities of our future together. I refused to be denied.

If by chance, Mr. Ferguson told me "No", I was determined to come back again and again and again and again until … his NO, became YES!

It appeared that I had passed the initial test because after that moment of silence, he didn't lose his mind and go slap crazy on me, nor did he go into the other room to get his handgun. Instead, he proceeded to ask me another question. That question was even more thought-provoking.

"Are you sure?" Mr. Ferguson questioned.

Then he looked over to a woman who sat alone off to the side – basically in the corner of the room. He continued, "Are you sure you want to marry my daughter? Because it is a good chance that she can end up like her." as he pointed to the woman in the corner.

THE WOMAN WHO SAT IN THE CORNER

Pure. Genuine. Love-filled. Reassurance. Every time I locked eyes with her, I could not help but be reassured that I was in the right place. There was a pure and genuine love that I felt. *Have you encountered someone that made you feel that way before?*

I mean… You had to be there (or at the very least you had to meet her for yourself) to fully understand why I admired this woman who sat in the corner the way I did.

She somehow gave you strength and hope even though she sat restricted to a wheelchair. You could see the physical toll that this hereditary, incurable disorder had on her. Yet when she smiled, you were inspired to smile despite the challenges and adversity faced. When her eyes connected with yours, you were given permission to embrace and enjoy every waking day that you were blessed to see.

Although she was small in stature, standing at four feet eleven inches, she was indeed a giant in character and leadership.

By definition, **character** *is the essence of a person.* It is who they are authentically. **Leadership** *is the ability to influence others.* This woman used her poise, her compassion, her wisdom, her joy, and her kindness to influence the lives of so many, including my own.

Alright, so who is this woman you ask?

Mrs. Eleanor Ferguson. They called her, Eleanor. She was the woman that sat in the corner. The one that Mr. Ferguson pointed to as he sought to test my resolve. She was Alexia's mother. In fact, the mother of all five of Mr. Ferguson's children.

EYES OF THE HEART

Mrs. Eleanor might have been wheelchair-bound, yet her love for people and her joy for life was unfettered.

She was a lady of few words, but her heart spoke volumes. The way to know her heart was through her eyes. Whether it was the sparkling glimmer or the soul-penetrating gaze, she had a way of letting her heart be heard.

Please don't get it twisted, Mrs. Eleanor did not say much because she didn't have anything to say – no. Actually, she was a natural-born nurturer who enjoyed people very much and encouraged them. If she could've talked, believe me she would have handed out plenty of life lessons and shared insightful wisdom. But Spinocerebellar Ataxia – the disorder that plagued the Sharp and Ferguson family – prevented her from verbally expressing herself.

Truth was, this merciless debilitation deprived her of simple joys like walking, dancing, and playing with her kids. Bathing, cooking, or combing her daughters' hair. Even the act of being heard and understood by others to include her own family was a frustrating reality for Mrs. Eleanor.

Physically, she was nearly incapable of talking. Unless you listened very carefully, each word seemed to be a groan. One that took much effort and energy to belt out. For her, talking was so laborious that it was easier to sit in silence at times. Quite frankly, sometimes deciphering her talks were just as taxing for the listener. By default, she was a woman of few words.

Yet if you sincerely focused on the eyes of her heart, you would perceive the message that Mrs. Eleanor desperately desired to share.

WORDS CAN'T EXPRESS

Although young, I was a high school senior who was mature beyond my years – so I was told. Now, I didn't profess to know everything. One thing I did know and two things for sure: (1) I was not born to fit in. (2) Anything worth doing was worth doing with everything I got.

I found it dissatisfying trying to fit in with everyone else. Truth-of-the-matter, I felt a little sick and embarrassed anytime I tried to blend in with the crowd. It rarely sat right with me to be like everyone else. I not only had to be different, but I had to go all out being different.

By different, I mean in my dress, my demeanor, and my decisions.

SIDE NOTE: *When you know that you are destined for greatness and are uniquely created to leave a peculiar mark on this world, you move, act, and think differently.*

I like to believe that this personal conviction justified my hunger for being different.

Therefore, when Mr. Ferguson asked me, "Are you sure?", without any hesitation, I emphatically replied, "YES … Sir! Mr. Ferguson, even if she ends up like her mama, I am not going anywhere. I love your daughter!"

Crazy. Stupid. Bold. That was me. I was crazy enough to be different. I was stupid enough to not care about how people felt about me being different. I was bold enough to stand by my decisions with little to no compromise.

Most of the guys I knew would have wasted no time bolting for the nearest exit if they knew that they got their girlfriend pregnant. They would have taken any excuse that came their way if it meant that they did not have to give up their freedom and be tethered to a woman and child. I was *not* that guy.

There are situations where your words are not enough. Your words can't express how committed you are to what you believe in. This was one of those situations in my life. Although I could not articulate it the way I felt it, I know that I could better explain with my actions.

UNTAPPED AND UNREALIZED

I am not sure who this message is for, but if you are reading this, I believe it is for you. If you do not take away anything else, please remember this: there's no promise made, great or small, that doesn't deserve to be fulfilled.

On that pursuit to fulfill your promise is where greatness resides. With every thought pondered, every act displayed, and every decision made in pursuit of making good on your promise, you will realize something extraordinary – that is the person that you became along the way.

Inside of each of us is potential. Potential to become all that we were created to be. Potential to do all that we were created to do. Sadly, for the majority of people, they will die with untapped and unrealized potential. Never becoming who they could have been and never doing all they could have done. Why is that?

Because they failed to place a demand on their potential. Had they made a promise to themselves and kept it, perhaps they could have enjoyed the fruit of completion – satisfaction.

BE WHO YOU SAY YOU ARE

One way that a person places a demand on potential is by making promises. When they set out to fulfill those promises, they inevitably tap into their potential. If you are the one that desires to win, I challenge you to make a promise that *you* will keep. Then keep the promise that *you* make.

I told my high school sweetheart that I would defend our love and that we would do this together. That was my promise to us.

At our high school graduation, I continued to make good on my promise. Immediately after I walked the stage and received my diploma, I located Alexia and escorted her to the center of the arena. While the remainder of my classmates waited in line to walk the stage and receive their diplomas, I crazily took my shot to prove to the love of my life that I was not going anywhere.

I got down on bended knee in front of thousands of people and asked her if she would allow me to make good on my promise to her for the rest of my life.

She said, "YES!" We hugged. We kissed. We celebrated. Then I went off to serve our country in the United States Marine Corps. Well fast forward to the day that I am writing this, Alexia and I are a few months away from celebrating our 22nd wedding anniversary. This is something that our parents did not model for us.

We have five amazing children. Two of which are adults – our daughter, the one that my wife was pregnant with in high school, is in the U.S. Marine Corps and the other is in his second year of college at his dream school, Texas Christian University (TCU). Two are high school scholars and student athletes. Our youngest is also a scholar and student athlete who is finishing her last year in junior high.

We are blazing a new trail and rewriting our family history, all because we remembered that there's no promise, great or small, that doesn't deserve to be fulfilled.

Now has there been challenges in our lives? Absolutely.

That same disorder that Mrs. Eleanor had, my wife and I discovered that she had it shortly after I was honorably discharged from the Corps. About six years into our marriage while pregnant with our third child, my wife started to lose her balance and fall. It was scary.

Eventually she would be bound to a wheelchair. Just like her mother, my wife's communication had been drastically limited. But if you sincerely keep your eyes on her heart, you will hear her joy for life and how deep her love runs for people. It is just as infectious as Mrs. Eleanor's.

It's one thing to say that you are going to win. It's another thing to win. But it is an entirely different thing to be the winner that you need to be to consistently win.

I don't want to downplay the power of words. They are very important especially when shaping the mindset. But there will come a time in your life [or perhaps it has already come] when mere words will not be enough to get you through the challenges and obstacles that stand in your way.

Understand that you are only as good as your word. The way that you and I are to honor our word is by our character.

Your word means nothing if you are not who you say you are.

Mrs. Eleanor taught me that if your words can't seem to express how you feel, the thoughts you're thinking, or what you deeply believe, that's okay as long as you are *being* it. That's most important!

CHARACTER SPEAKS LOUDEST

Never mind the adage, *your actions speak louder than words.* Far louder than your words or even your actions, your character speaks the loudest. That's why it is critically important that we persistently focus our attention on the eyes of our heart. There lie the clues for our next do-it-yourself project.

For every level that we desire to reach, there is a DIY project that we must complete. Maybe for one level it is self-identity. You may need to work on knowing who you are. On another level, it may be forgiveness. Because of past traumas or hardships, you may have developed insecurities about yourself or distrust for people. You must forgive to move on. Other levels may be preserving your worth. You work on adopting certain disciplines or establishing certain boundaries.

I am not sure what your do-it-yourself project entails, but I am convinced that none of us will escape this world without first being presented with it. Regardless of what it is, know that it is there to help you tap into your greatest potential. That is being a winner!

Winning isn't hard but it is work.

Which simply means that anyone who desires to win and is committed to the process can look up one day and realize that they are a success story. But it cannot and will not happen aside from work. Your level of work depends squarely on who you become – your character.

KEEP YOUR EYES ON THE HEART

Here's my desire for you - that your convictions will cause you to stand ten-toes-flat by the promises you make so you can one day enjoy the fruit of a fulfilled promise – the winning you. All you have to do is keep your eyes on the heart.

Say it loud:

I AM A WINNER! AND TODAY... I WIN!

ABOUT THE AUTHOR:

Social Media:
IG @1darrylwthomas
FB @1darrylwthomas
LinkedIn: @1darrylwthomas
Email darrylwthomasjr@gmail.com

Darryl W. Thomas, Jr. is a U.S. Marine Corps Veteran with more than 20 years of experience helping young adults transform trauma into triumph. Darry is a certified Life Coach and Master Communicator, and the CEO and Senior At-Risk Interventionist of Committed 2 Win, LLC (a personal and leadership development company).

Darryl is a former at-risk student who witness the tragic passing of his father as a high school freshman and endured the abandonment of his mother suffered from drug abuse. Not only has Darryl defied all odds, but he has also made it his life's purpose to coach leadership and character education to underserved youth in secondary and post-secondary education.

He has gone from training military troops to coaching leadership and character to the next generation of leaders in post-secondary education. Darryl's empowering message and communication style resonates with diverse groups of first generation, low-income & disabled college students including Baylor University, McLennan Community College, Faith & Sports Institute (FSI), HBCU Rising Mentors, Advancement Via Individual Determination (AVID) plus more.

Darryl is a 3x Amazon Best-Selling Author as well as an International Best-Selling Author. His most notable publishing is his personal memoir entitled, TODAY... I WIN: When Tests Go Beyond The Classroom.

He and his phenomenal wife believe whole-heartedly that a candle loses nothing by lighting another candle. His primary focus in life is to impact generational transformation.

Darryl's personal mission is to help transform 1 million young people into leaders of change starting with his five children and the young kings and queens that he and his team mentor at the The Size Of a Man – 501(c)3 organization dedicated to breaking the cycles of fatherlessness and poverty. Simply put, Darryl is convinced that a person is purposed to win as long as they don't quit.

SERVICES OFFERED AT COMMITTED 2 WIN

Student Conferences & Workshops
Leadership Camps
Reading Literacy Programs
Educational Consultation
Staff Development Workshops
Leadership & Character Development Programs (school based & SEL curriculum)
Keynote Presentations (commencements, convocations, student assemblies, etc.)

KEYNOTE TOPICS INCLUDE:

GRIT: The Art of Being Faithful to Your Commitment
Suicide Prevention
Leveraging Your Imagination for Success
Winning on Purpose
No More Distractions & Insecurities: Eliminating the Noise
Mastering the Way You Talk

LOVE IS WINNING
Derrick Pearson

The Conversation in your head.

In baseball, it is the 3-2 pitch with 2 outs. What is the score? What is my best pitch? What pitch can I handle? Where are they playing me? In basketball, it is the free throw attempt to give your team the lead. Take a deep breath. Dry my hands. Who do I need to box out? What defense are we in? What do I do next? In football, it is 4th down in the 4th quarter, and you need one yard to lock up the game. What is our best short yardage play? Do I have the right personnel on the field? What is our strength? Who is our best player? Where do we have an advantage? In hockey and soccer, it is the penalty shot, one on one for the game and your legacy. Where will I line up? What am I going to attack? What shots have I made before in a shootout? What does the goalie do best? Top shelf? Pump fake? In life, it is the moment before the presentation or the elevator ride to the floor where financial dreams come true. Am I prepared? Did I rehearse this enough? Do I know what they want to hear? Am I ready to tell them what they need to know?

Your mindset is the place where these conversations happen, and it is the place where decisions are made, and direction is determined. It doesn't matter if you call it your outlook, ethos, world view, ideology, or mentality, it is in the conversation that you have with yourself where winning is focused in on. It is in those conversations where focus, purpose, mission, and value are put on display. To have a successful mindset, we determine what is in play, what is to be avoided, and what is the end result we are seeking. A winning mindset requires that we determine what winning is, and then what is required for it to happen.

Winning. Two people or groups can achieve the same basic result, but not both consider it a win. Details are required. A player can end up on third base but not have the same value in getting there. Winning is relative. Did you achieve the most important thing? Did you score more points than you usually do but give up more as well? Did you have your best game but not get the best result? Are you satisfied? Are you done? Did you succeed?

Some of the teams that I coached won 100% of the games played, and some of them won 25%. Overall, my players won 78 percent of the games that I coached. There is a phrase that most know that some disagree with. "Win or learn. Never lose." I will say that I agree with it. My teams won 78 percent of the games played. We learned how to win in those other 22 percent. We got better after each lesson. We remember the lessons at a much deeper level than we remember the wins. I also never coached to win. I coached to love and lead, on the field and off. The successes on the field should match the love. That was my mindset. Love. Lead through love to the best version of ourselves.

I coach with a GPS in mind. At the beginning of each season, I would determine who my players were, what kind of love would be required to make them better on the field and off, and then what love I wanted them covered in at and by seasons end. Daunting task for sure, but improvement requires love greater than the friction faced. Coaching mindset rule: Love first, love last, and in between, love more.

Love first. Meeting yourself and your players where they currently are. What is the location? Where are you determined how far you have come and how far you had to go. If we won three games and had 3 student athletes who achieved a 3.5 GPA or higher or had one leader and needed three. Do we have talent but no heart? Are we skilled but have no focus? What if we are physically gifted but easily distracted?

Love last. Where are we going? What does success look like? How far away is this goal? Do we plan to win 50 percent of our games? Do we need to win 75 percent of them? Can we? Are we committed and disciplined enough to win them all? What should our team GPA be? What will make the community connect? What will make the parents proud? Where will this take these student athletes in the future?

And in between, love more. Location has been identified. Mission and final destination has been set into the programs GPA. Now, we need to choose how we are to get there. (Pay attention to the coaching mindset) Love first, love last, and in between…LOVE MORE. Care enough to put boundaries in place for the sake of team connection and accountability. Care enough to honestly determine where you are, who you are, and what the goals and missions are. Where we are lets the GPS reminds us if we are on time and on mission. If a distraction occurs, the GPS will loudly state that it appears that we are drifting away from the end mission and focus. It will ask if we are sure that this is the path we want to take and if we would like to reroute. Reroutes happen all the time. You originally stated that 100 percent was your mission, but your actions appear to he headed directly towards 60 percent. Pay attention to the path. The GPS will notify you of roadblocks and detours. Do not ignore them. "It appears that we are idling. Is this true?" "You have veered off course from winning, would you like to recalculate?"

I refuse to say that one team that I coached was better than another, but I can say that some teams tested this mindset of winning more than others. One was a baseball team in Virginia, and this team needed a GPS in the worst way. They were a rudderless ship in a storm of raging waves. I was asked to come on board, save the ship, or at least try to save the cargo. Location: Middle of the Atlantic during the worst storm I had ever seen. The ship was tattered and worn. A team of 13 young men who were holding on for dear life. I had no idea who they were or how they got to where they were. I had two days before the final exhibition game, and I had not seen them play. I called one of my most trusted coaching friends and begged him to come help. This coach had recently helped me at a different school, and we had had great success there. I warned him that this program did not have the talent, quantity, or quality of players that we had just left, but I thought they had the heart to hang on in a tough situation. That showed up when their leader left, and that told me that they cared. That would be what we coached from. Caring.

Jason Hoskins showed up and we evaluated the team. We shook our heads and sighed deep sighs often. They strolled through indoor batting cage session after session. There was effort but not much success. We were left notes from the previous coach, so we took those notes as gospel. Being that we had little time to prepare them for the exhibition in two days. We were told who the starters should be at each position, who the reserves should be, and what they had been taught so far. We had two days.

Two days later, the team prepared to board the bus for our first exhibition game. The players were in various degrees of dress and unpreparedness. The wrong type of shoes, gloves that had not been broken in, hats worn wrong, and not a smile to be seen. Its as if they were trying to warn us that this wasn't going to be good. It wasn't. We faced a powerhouse squad and program, and they looked the part. I watched them warm up to perfection. Perfect form, timely chatter, good energy, competent athletic movement, and impeccable uniforms. We could not go four throws without the player missing the throw or a player bouncing it three times before it could get to its recipient. We took a brutal round of batting practice, and a tougher round of infield. Before the game, I like to take a few pitches from my starter so that I can see what type of stuff he has. It helps with calling pitches. It lets me know If they are hitting their spots, what the velocity is, and how their mechanics are going.

I checked my notes from the previous coach on the starter. "Innings eater, won't throw hard but will throw strikes." Great. I can work with that. The only bad pitch is a ball. We can't defend it. The pregame bullpen session went as follows: ball in the dirt, ball over my head, ball in the dirt, ball over my head, and repeat. Find love. I called him over and asked how he was doing. "Fine. As usual. I usually do better in games." Whew. Good.

First inning, he takes the mound and proceeds to throw 31 pitches. I believe that 24 were balls. The other seven got hit to the fence or past a flailing infielder. It was 12-0 before I could save him from himself. I walked out to the mound and smiled as I took the baseball from him. I looked for another option, and there was not one set of eyes that were purposefully trying to meet mine. We lost that game 31-0 in five innings. The bus ride home might as well have been a bus ride to the dentist. Jason and I knew that the following practice would speak volumes. Who would show up after this? If they didn't show up, we would understand.

Monday came, and all 13 players showed up. I asked them why and they said that they wanted to learn how to play. They wanted to be proud of themselves. We put the gloves and bats away and talked. We found out who they were, why they played, and what they knew and didn't know. They told us everything. Their fears, dreams, passions, and families. We told them that we heard them and cared. The next day, we went to work. A total demolition of bad habits and negative thinking. We had to renovate their minds, erasing bad memories, and we framed lessons so that we could play smarter. We could play from love of the game and each other rather than hearing the negative comments and doubts.

We taught and re-taught them to throw, warm up, catch, hit, stand, sit, and talk. We celebrated the steps, the mistakes forward, and the effort. We celebrated the love of the game, which was reinforced by the conversations we had with each other and ourselves. We make it okay to love the game and ourselves. We also celebrated each day. Each lesson in class. Each victory for exams. Each effort in study hall. Each family mission and each community highlight. These young men celebrated smiles and stalked them in their day-to-day activities. They smiled at each other, at their teachers and classmates, and their opponents. They forgot to be miserable, and in the meanwhile, they forgot to lose. They learned. In that learning, they began to win. This ragtag team that gave up 31 runs and then learned its way to a 6-game losing streak began winning. This team won 6 of its last 8 games, including beating several teams that bettered them earlier. This team also became leaders in the classrooms, hallways, and streets of their city. At seasons end, they had changed themselves and the program, the school and their homes, and their grades and hearts.

What changed? Mindset. With location, mission, and path identified, they were able to talk to themselves about the result. Happiness. Joy. Pride. Confidence. Knowledge. They had learned to enjoy the process by creating a climate where the voices spoke well of them, to them, about them. They took each step with a common voice of positive direction in their heads. Coaching vibe: Hear something good, see something good, say something good. Coaching chant: Love Out Loud. AMPLIFY THE GOOD SILENCE THE BAD. Coaching question: What did you win? What did you learn?

This may have been the best coaching I have ever done. Jason Hoskins was at his best, lifting the lowest to the highest, shining light in the darkest of spaces and places. Winning was moment by moment, action by action, drill by drill, and success after success. We never talked about the game results because we knew that focusing on the result would lessen the joy of the process. We never talked about grades because it would put the focus on the last thing and cheapen the next thing. THE LESSON. The goal was 3.5 via daily efforts, singular efforts, and celebrated efforts along the way. Celebrate April Monday and you will get to celebrate May Monday when it has been done well. Honor the lesson on Monday and it will give value to the exam on Friday. Love your teacher as she teaches instead of after they are done. Tell your parents everything, good and bad, right, and wrong, victory or lesson. They deserve to learn too.

The best part of this is the love. I can say that I loved every team that I ever played on this way. We got the same results from the same love, and no matter if this was in Texas, Virginia, Utah, or Nebraska, loving first always worked. Loving last always worked. Loving in between was always the right path, reason, and explanation. Loving in between was the best boundary I could dream of. The constant comfort of knowing that the conversation in my head was good for the sender and the receiver made the journey a better journey. A more loving journey.

No matter the sport, each has its own moments of unity and isolation. Each has its conversation places. The huddle, the pitcher's mound, the locker room, and the bus. In those places, the conversations in your head have a lot of impact of the results of the games connected to them. In those conversations, I choose to connect and reconnect, direct and redirect, love and re-love. "How are we doing?" What do you see?" What do you want to do next?" "Are you having fun yet?"

As you read this, I hope that the conversation in your head leads you to a more loving conversation with yourself. Embrace the friction. Celebrate the lesson. Love yourself no matter the result. That is winning. That is the good mindset. Understand your environment and situation. Take your next forward step. Go. Celebrate. That is the winning mindset. Setting your own personal GPS for whatever it is you are doing next. Where are you now? Where are you going? How will you get there?

Whatever the question is in your head, the winning mindset has an answer to them all. Love. Love. And in between, more love.

ABOUT THE AUTHOR:

Social Media:
IG @derrickpearson
FB @derrick.pearson.5
LinkedIn: @derrick-pearson-b5580524
Email pearsonderrick@aol.com

Derrick Pearson- Sports Radio Station Owner KNTK-FM Lincoln, Nebraska. Co-Host "Old School with Jay Foreman" "DP One on One" at 93.7 The Ticket FM Lincoln, Nebraska. Speaker-TEDxLander May 2019. The love Project Speaker-TEDxDeerPark March 2020. An American Face 3X Amazon Best Selling Author "The Impact of Influence, (Volumes 1,2, 4) Rebuilt Through Recovery

Derrick "DP" Pearson DP has spent stops during his career as a sportscaster, radio and television host, writer, manager and high school coach. That career has taken him nationwide, including Washington, DC, Charlotte, Los Angeles, Salt Lake City, and Atlanta. In addition to his media and coaching ventures, he also helped establish Fat Guy Charities in Charlotte, an NFL Charity, and developed LovePrints, a national mentor program that promotes Loving and Learning through Sports. DP joins Jay Foreman every weekday from 8:00 am – 10:00 am. One on One with DP airs weekdays from 10:00 – 11:00 each weekday morning.

SUCCESS MEANS SACRIFICE
Deuce Malone

When I was approached to be a part of this project, I was filled with immense pleasure because this is a subject that I love to talk about. My name is Deuce Malone and I am a veteran in the music industry with over twenty years of experience. Yes, over twenty years. Now, that might sound like an amazing career full of glitz, glamour, red carpets, and elaborate parties. And you would be right, partially. What people don't see about the music industry is the sacrifice that it takes to maintain a lengthy career. So, let's dive in.

My career first began as a dream. I would picture myself on stages with crowds cheering my name. I envisioned myself having songs on the top of the Billboard 200 chart. But how was I supposed to get there? In my mind, all I needed to do was to create a song, because I had the talent. So I begin the creative process.

I would write songs using instrumentals from the songs that were played on the radio. I would go to the music stores at the mall and buy albums and singles and read the liner notes to see who worked on those songs and then research those people. It became my obsession to learn as much as I could about how my favorite songs were made and how I could recreate that process by my own means. By researching the people involved, I could then have a place to mail, yes mail, my demo songs to those people in hopes of getting signed to a big record label.

I was a teenager when I began this musical journey. Probably around thirteen or fourteen. While most teenagers were playing with their friends, going to sleepovers, and school dances. I was consumed with using my spare time to stay connected to music. Sacrifice. It was a non-negotiable for me to make sure I was home every day at 4 pm to watch Rap City on BET. If it was during football season and I had practice, I would make sure I taped Rap City and watched it when I got home. I did the same with Yo MTV Raps. I kept issues of The Source and XXL in my book bag to read at lunch or on the bus to and from school.

This was my research and foundation to get to the next level. I was consumed by the music and entertainment industry. And it began to show to those around me. In my school, I became the guy people went to ask what were the hottest songs coming out at that time. When you dig into your passion, people will begin to notice, because it emanates from you. You will gravitate to conversations involving your passions. You will let pieces of your passion flow into your normal vocations. And people will notice. You will become a thought leader when your area of passion comes up and people will look to you for your input. That's when you know you are doing the right thing.

To keep your position in your passion, you have to continue to sacrifice though. The day you slack, you allow someone else the opportunity to overtake you. I don't know about you, but I refuse to let anyone outshine me. So I continue, to this day to sacrifice. I managed to graduate high school with honors and be known as the guy who was deeply involved in music. I didn't get that record deal I dreamed about, but I did record a few songs with some friends I formed a rap group with. I moved on to Texas State University after graduation. And guess what, I didn't let a new town, new environment stop me from my dreams. I found the closest record store that I could find, Sundance Music, and it became my new hangout place. I would be there every Tuesday when new albums came out. Eventually, I would meet the man who honestly set my career on the right path. Greg Williams.

Greg was a journalism major, rapper, and DJ. Those last two instantly connected us. While most of my peers were going to frat parties, clubbing, and oversleeping their 8 am classes—we would have freestyle sessions in one of our dorms. Don't get me wrong, I went to quite a few parties in college, but every Tuesday from 10 pm until, we would make music. Eventually, we connected with some other gentlemen who were into music and we started a collective called The Word Association. I like to call us the Wu-Tang of San Marcos, TX. Every Tuesday the Word Association would freestyle, create tracks, and figure out a way for us to make it in the music business.

I hope you've been paying attention to my story so far. And if you have, you may have noticed I haven't mentioned anything about me making money, going to any cool parties, or anything glamorous happening. Because at that time, there weren't any. You see, on the way to success, it takes a lot of long nights with no payoff. A lot of long days with minimal to no profit. If you're a musician, you may do shows for free. You end up using the money you save to buy equipment to help the pursuit of your dream easier. It's not a cakewalk, but that is why you need to have a winning mindset and understand that the sacrifices you make today, will pay off tomorrow. Even if that tomorrow is ten to fifteen years in the future.

In my senior year of college, I would take over Greg's on-campus radio show. Greg graduated a semester earlier than me and gave me a shot to keep the only hip-hop-related genre on the college station. I jumped at the opportunity. I saw this as another way to learn more about a different aspect of the music industry and maybe even play some of my own music. This was an unpaid gig. No money. Not even college credit. And the show was every Friday night. So instead of hitting the bars or making a trip to see my folks in Austin earlier, I would hone my skills as a radio DJ. Little did I know that this would actually be prepping me for the career that would take me to the next level.

When I graduated from Texas State University, I had two things on my mind. Get a job and have that job fund my music passions.

My thought process was that I could get a job in my major and make some good money to afford more equipment and buy studio time. That sounded like a great plan. But upon graduating I had no lucrative job offers to accept. By pure luck, I did have a friend from college that had started working at a new radio station in Austin. She already had her own show and knew the station needed people to work on the promotions team. She also knew how much I loved music and that I did some college radio so fitting in at the station would be easy. Now, radio promotions people didn't get paid hardly any money in those days. We're talking barely above minimum wage and the hours were sporadic. Your job as a promo person was to go to events and pass out T-shirts and stickers to listeners of the radio station. Let's recap this situation so you fully understand. At this point and time, I am a fresh college graduate and instead of continuing to try to get a corporate job, I am considering taking a job paying above minimum wage by passing out stickers?

I took the job. I took the job because once again I saw it as an opportunity to learn more and be around the music industry. I also knew this was a different ball game. This was corporate radio. This was where any major artist coming into Austin would stop by to do interviews with the on-air DJs. My thought was if I'm in the building at least I could maybe meet a few artists and pass my music along to them.

In a matter of six months of me working as a promotions person and stepping in wherever the radio station needed someone to fill in a shift, I was given the chance to try out to be a weekend DJ. The Program Director of the station had heard about my college radio experience and saw me constantly being around the station working and gave me a shot. After my first few weekend shifts, I was given a permanent weekend spot on Saturday nights. I felt like I had "made it." My friends from high school were hearing me on the radio and calling in. the main DJs were giving me a little more respect because I was no longer one of the promotions guys, but was now in their ranks. The lesson here is sometimes you have to swallow your pride and look at the big picture. I took a job for low pay while living with my Mom, to learn and soak up as much as I could about an industry I was passionate about. Most people won't do those things and that is why they stay in a position they don't want to be in. People notice dedication and drive and will reward those who earn it. And earn it I did.

Full-time radio jobs are few and far between. There are only four full-time radio jobs on any station that you listen to in America. Mornings, Middays, Afternoons, and Nights. If you are a radio DJ and you are in a smaller city, your job options are very limited because there are probably not going to be a lot of radio stations. If you only want to work in a specific genre, that makes your options even slimmer. To get the opportunity at a full-time spot, you are going to have to either move, hope that a full-time DJ moves, or gets fired. In my case, someone got fired.

The nighttime DJ at the station, who I considered a mentor, was unexpectedly fired and I was asked to fill in for him. The nighttime DJ slot is the time when most of the school-age kids and party people are listening to the radio. These DJs are typically the "coolest" and "hippest" people on a radio station. Filling in definitely had my nerves a bit shook, but this was no different than my dream, just a different pathway to get there.

After a few weeks, the station decided to officially give me the job. I was now a full-time on-air DJ on a commercial radio station in one of the largest cities in Texas. Let me catch you up to speed. I graduated from college, took a risk in a low-paying job, worked my tail off, and caught the eye of the suits and when the opportunity presented itself, I executed. All within an eight-month time frame. That's the way you have to approach your dreams and passion. Look at the overall opportunity and see how the options fit into your dream and work your tail off.

Do you remember what I told you my passion was? I wanted to be on-stages and have songs on Billboard charts and work in the music industry right. Well, radio made me choose where my path was going to take me. By taking the on-air gig, I wouldn't have the time to continue being in the Word Association full time. However, the radio job put me in front of the biggest artists in hip hop literally every week. I put my music-making career on hold to a degree to dive deep into radio. I focused on building a show that built the basis for what a career would grow to be. My show became the number one night show in Austin for six years straight. During that time, I interviewed, and sometimes even became friends with, the top players in the music industry. You can take a look at my social media, @TheWorldOfDeuce on all platforms, to see some faces you may recognize.

For me, it wasn't just the celebrities though. I was meeting the managers, the record label reps, the agents, and more. These were the people who made the industry move. Seeing how radio functioned within the industry and learning from record label people gave me all the game I needed to truly know how to market and promote my own music. And I then had the network to get music into the right hands even faster.

One night while I was out DJing one of my club nights for the radio, I bumped into a guy in the bar. I spilled his drink even! I offered to buy the guy a drink and we began chatting about things. He was an artist. My thought was "of course." I met artists every day because everyone always wanted me to play their music. But this guy was different though and we had a lot in common from our conversation. We exchanged numbers and kept in contact from that day forward. Who would figure that a spilled drink would cause a relationship to form that would lead to me and this individual being at the Grammys years later? That individual is the producer and artist known as TROY NōKA. Let me give him a proper introduction. GRAMMY award-winning producer, rapper, writer, husband, and father. He's produced for the likes of Doja Cat, John Legend, Ciara, The Backstreet Boys, Frank Ocean, and Miguel to name a few. And I just so happen to be the President of his label Wiz Up Entertainment.

When radio ended for me in 2009, the contacts I had made over my years in the industry allowed me to pivot into the artist management and festival realm. TROY and I begin making plans on how to further his career and how to also impact other artists' careers. I even started working for a festival here in Austin, for free, to learn more about festival management and promotion. Yes, you read that correctly, I worked for a festival for free to learn. That's the winning mindset. Seeing an opportunity and taking full advantage to learn. The information that I gained from the festival added another item to my musical resume. The kid who had dreams of being on Billboard and working in the music industry stayed true to his passion and found ways to always work at his craft. For minimal pay, big checks, or for free. I, like you, have to put in the work for your passion and not complain.

If there is nothing else that you take from my story, then take this. When you aim to get 1% better at your passion every day and surround yourself with like-minded individuals working toward the same goal, you will achieve what you want. The funny thing is, it may not 100% materialize the way you envisioned it, but you will get there. I literally wanted to be the one on the stage as the star, but I ended up being the one building the stage and the artists to make the show happen. It's my dream with a twist. Now go after your dream and send me a message at theworldofdeuce@gmail.com when you achieve it!

ABOUT THE AUTHOR:

Social Media:
IG @theworldofdeuce
FB @theworldofdeuce
LinkedIn: @deucemalone
Email deuce@theworldofdeuce.com

Deuce Malone is a twenty-year music industry vet with experience in retail, FM radio, artist management, festival organization, deejaying, and as an artist. Currently, Deuce serves as President of Wiz Up Entertainment, home of GRAMMY award-winning producer TROY NōKA he is also the CEO of Hustle My Religion apparel, and a member of the Recording Academy of America. In his spare time, Deuce is an avid gamer and sneakerhead with over 150 sneakers in his personal collection.

He is also a huge sports fan. He supports all teams from his hometown in the Houston area –especially the Houston Rockets. You can also find him at most University of Texas Longhorn football and basketball games.

Deuce lives by the phrase, "Emotions will leave you broke."

Broke—as in emotionally hurt, and broke—as in penniless. He strives to act with integrity and temper emotions at all times. Bringing a smile to others' faces is what makes him happy. You can find Deuce online on all social media platforms under @TheWorldOfDeuce and in the live music capital of the world, Austin, TX.

MENTAL ROOTS
Ereka Howard

We all have a winning mindset. Sometimes it takes extra time to initiate it. There are some who need assistance in finding that mindset while others have the desire for a positive mindset. Oftentimes, we are not willing to do the work. In order to have a winning mindset, there needs to be room for failure. Think about it this way, how will we know how to ride a bike if we never fall while learning?

To incorporate mental health within a "Winning Mindset", there are a lot of different factors to consider if you have a potential mental illness. In detail, depression can have a huge impact on staying positive. For example, the behaviors within depression look and feel like a silent attack. Depression can come from the following areas.

- Genetics - One of the most influential factors in the onset of major depression is based on your genetic code.
- Substance Abuse - early childhood experiences or even major life events (Both Immediate and Prolonged).

Research shows that depression affects an estimated one in fifteen adults (6.7%) in any given year. One in six people (16.6%) will experience depression at some time in their life. Depression can occur at any time, but on average, first appears during the late teens to mid-twenties. Did you know that women are more likely than men to experience depression? This is a very alarming statement to think about, but it is true.

Failure does not determine who or what you represent in life. Failure is success turned inside out. A winning mindset requires failure. I remember when I had to take the state licensing board exam. After the fourth time of not passing, I completely gave up on the dream of being licensed. It made me feel inferior to all my other colleagues who are licensed. Shame, guilt, rejection, and anger were emotions that I had to accept.

To have a winning mindset, you must be ok with failure. True success resides in the ability to take ownership of the things you did not accomplish. Many people become so accustomed to failure that it stops them from achieving due to a lack of determination. True determination is a result of persevering further than those who gave up in life.

THE CYCLE OF THOUGHTS AND BEHAVIORS

Here's a closer look at how thoughts and emotions can influence behavior in a positive or negative way:

• Inaccurate, negative perceptions, or thoughts contribute to emotional distress and mental health concerns.

• These thoughts sometimes lead to unhelpful or harmful behaviors.

• Eventually, these thoughts and resulting behaviors can become a pattern that repeats itself.

• Learning how to address and change these patterns can help you deal with problems as they arise, which can help reduce future distress.

Typical treatment often involves the following:
• recognizing how inaccurate thinking can worsen problems
• learning new problem-solving skills
• gaining confidence and a better understanding and appreciation of your self-worth
• learning how to face fears and challenges

- using role play and calming techniques when faced with potentially challenging situations

What should you do if you are lacking the motivation to stay positive? As stated above, one way to do so is to cognitively restructure your thoughts. Before you do this, consider some underlying factors that might be the cause for your negative mindset. Let's define what cognitive restructuring is. This involves looking at any cognitive distortions affecting your thoughts such as black-and-white thinking, jumping to conclusions, or catastrophizing and beginning to unravel them. According to google, cognitive restructuring is a technique that has been successfully used to help people change the way they think. When used for stress management, the goal is to replace stress-producing thoughts (cognitive distortions) with more balanced thoughts that do not produce stress. In my own words, this means that we must be able to reshape our previous thoughts about a particular situation and experience. It's not always easy to do, but once it's done, you're golden. In conclusion, a winning mindset is something that takes time to own. We can be motivated one day and the next lack the same motivation that we once had before we "failed" at something. Whatever your reason is, know that you too can have a winning mindset once you put your mind to it.

ABOUT THE AUTHOR:

Social Media:
IG @msmotivational
FB @erekahowardmotivationalspeaker
LinkedIn: @mserekahoward
Email mserekahoward@gmail.com

Ms. Ereka Howard is no one-dimensional sensation.

She is a speaker, co-author, Certified Life Coach, Clinician, and Adoptee. Since the precocious age of eight, Ms. Ereka Howard has graced and impacted audiences throughout the nation alongside her adoptive mother. Ms. Ereka Howard has been recognized as an authority on motivation, peak performance, and peer leadership which has made her well respected amongst her community and audience. Ms. Ereka Howard creates an authentic connection with her audience as they think, laugh, applaud and remain engaged. Due to her ability to relate to and transform people's lives, she is a highly regarded nationally sought-after speaker. Ms. Ereka Howard displays knowledge, wisdom, and engaging speaking styles riddled with humor and captivating stories which have made her an asset to partnerships and audiences. After overcoming many hurdles throughout her life, Ms. Ereka Howard now shares her life experiences and teaches the community how to be successful throughout life. Ms. Ereka Howard has dedicated her life to the empowerment of everyone. She is a fresh voice for a new generation. Ms. Ereka Howard has a Bachelor of Science in Exercise and Sports Science and a Master in Clinical Mental Health Counseling. Ereka is currently working on a Doctorate in Counseling Education and Supervision.

WHAT IS THE REAL SECRET TO WINNING?
Hoss Tabrizi

When I was asked to contribute to this book, it was during a hectic point in my life. With my nine-year-old, I discussed the opportunity to share my mindset with readers. Without hesitation, Maximus emphatically explained, "you always preach about the winning mindset to us, so you must get your message out to more people." Alas, here we are.

Some of you are reading this because you want to have the winning mindset. To do so, you will need to learn what is the real secret to winning. You will learn more about the four keys to a winning mindset throughout the chapter: Have a goal in mind, Be resilient, Work hard until you achieve your goal, and Learn and grow.

When I was a kid, I learned a lot of life lessons through sports while watching greatness. Kobe Bryant, Magic Johnson, Jerry Rice, and Michael Jordan all had a certain edge to them that other athletes did not. What separated these elite athletes from the rest was their mindset. These great players never thought they were going to lose. These great players never thought they would lose because of their preparation. These great players prepared to the point no one could outwork them.

Before we dive into the real secret of winning, I'd like to propose a question. Do you consider yourself a winner? There are three answers that typically come from this: "No", "I'm not sure", and "YESSSSS".

What if I told you we are all winners?

For those of you that are unsure about your winning status, reading this book will hopefully give you clarity on how to become a winner.

If I were to bet, those that answered YESSSSS probably have more losses than the rest of you. They just have a better view of the scoreboard. I love the mindset, and I always hope it is there. I can tell you though - it's not. You have the ability to change a negative to a positive quickly. Or treat a loss as a lesson instead of defeat. These are important skills to have in order to "win."

This is who I am, and this is why winning matters to me - what I would like for you to do today is to shift your lenses on the scoreboard.

To be a winner, you must know what a winner is. Which of the following makes you a winner?

Raising a child	Being a doctor or lawyer
Being better than yesterday	Having a relationship with God
Having 10 million dollars in net worth	Owning a Jet
Donating regularly	Having a multi-million-dollar home
Protector from bullies	Serving your county
Owning an expensive car	Leading with love
Saving someone's life	

My six-year-old daughter, Mia, has a winning mindset. She's undefeated. One night at dinner, I asked her to give an example of a winning mindset, and she brought up the time she ran sprints against her nine-year-old brother, Maximus. To give a little background, Maximus is exceptionally fast in short distances. He's also a foot taller and more than double the weight of his little sister. If they were to race 100 times at 20 yards, he should win 100 times. The first five times they raced, he won all five times. It was supposed to only be five races. Mia, never defeated, said let's do 10 races. Determined to come back, the scoreboard read seven wins for Maximus, one win for Mia, and two ties. Mia changed it to the first to 10 wins. Again, she had no business even being close to her brother. He should have beaten her by a couple yards each race. But her mindset didn't care about that. She eventually "lost" 10 to five with five ties. Mia's winning mindset did not let her record this as a loss even though Maximus and the actual scoreboard did. Her mindset recorded this as a time where she had to get better and practice more. Her explanation that I am going to outwork him between now and the next race and beat him in that race is what the winning mindset is all about.

I used to teach summer school math in 2007 before I became a high school math teacher. There was a quote from John Wooden that was hung on the wall of my classroom that read, "Everyone fails in life. What you do next shows your composition." For students to be in summer school, they had all "failed" during their previous attempt of the course. These students thought they were "failures". Most of their parents thought they were "failures". Their previous teachers thought they were "failures". What a terrible feeling, and it wasn't just one kid, but 24 kids. Add up the parents and teachers and that's a lot of negative attitudes that needed correction.

The mission I made for myself was: not only do the students need to pass the course, and required state exam, but learn that they could overcome any obstacle if they put their mind to it. Some of these kids failed for multiple years and had gotten low scores on their state exams. It was my duty to pass on my winning mindset to these students. Challenge accepted!

It wasn't easy. It took hard work. It took perseverance. It took each student learning that they were not failures, but gifted and needed to see and hear things differently in order to be successful.

All the students passed the course and state exams. Because of this, they graduated high school after completing this requirement. I enjoyed the moment back in 2007. I saw the confidence that came from "winning," but the biggest reward came to me 10 to 15 years later when a couple of those students found me to tell me about their careers and how great their lives were. It was very rewarding to be able to pass on my winning mindset in this instance.

My physical health is my kryptonite. I have an MRI machine named after me based on how many exams I have had. I had to give up contact sports in 2006 based on my history of concussions and traumatic brain injuries that I obtained prior to 2006. Now, I play tennis. However, with the way I play tennis, I tend to get injured often. I obsess over recovery and my physical health. My health was always a priority, and I spent lots of time doing physical therapy as well as exercise and rehabilitation because "losing" when it came to my health was never acceptable to me. Despite all this, I was injured again in the spring of 2022. My spine will most likely cause issues along my cervical, thoracic, and lumbar spine as well as my hips and all the muscles near those regions. Since I like winning, I decided to take control of something else. My weight. Weight gain during covid and injuries that prevented me from exercising caused me to balloon to 225 pounds. I was determined to lose weight by eating correctly and winning via nutrition. We came up with a goal of getting down to 190 pounds. I had to do this. I hired a nutritionist, and we came up with a plan. It wasn't easy. I had my ups and downs, but my big belly that rivaled Santa Claus started to show some muscles. There was no way I was going to give up because of my winning mindset. I kept working to eventually win.

In these stories, hopefully you saw the secret to obtaining a winning mindset. There are four keys to having a winning mindset:

1. Have a goal in mind.

What happens when you don't have a goal in mind? You don't have a constant reminder that could help lift you during difficult times. If a goal is a team goal for sports, like winning a super bowl, it may elevate how you practice or deal with losses. There are plenty of teams that do not go undefeated that still win a championship. Was their season over after their first loss a couple games into the season? No. There are numerous teams that didn't win their division that went on to win a championship. Are those teams' losers since they didn't win their division? No. The larger goal of winning a championship is what mattered most. The "losses" aren't what's remembered at the end of the season. The last team standing is what's etched in stone.

When I want to achieve something in life, I need to identify what that is and constantly think about it. I need to break down what I'm trying to accomplish into small, attainable goals while keeping the larger goal in mind. For example, going from 225 pounds to 190 pounds seems daunting. Losing 35 pounds isn't easy. However, losing six pounds a month for six months is achievable. An even less daunting goal is to lose 1.5 pounds a week, further broken down into a daily number of a 750 calories deficit compared to what's needed to maintain your weight.

2. Be resilient.

Imagine a rock being placed inside of a rubber band. The further the band is pulled back the further the rock will go. At some point, the rubber band will break. Those with resiliency are like a rubber band that will never break. And if you push or pull them really far, they are going to come out firing with lots of velocity.

There are going to be obstacles or hiccups along the way when trying to obtain your goal. Your mind plays an important role in what happens next. My oldest son dislikes running long distances.

81

I do as well. There is this large hill near the middle of a run that we do that makes the run difficult. My mindset is I'm going to crush this annoying hill and then the rest of the run is downhill and easy. I've taught my son to focus on other things during the run instead of the voice that tells him to start walking. For one minute, we focus on pumping our arms. For the next minute, we focus on getting one foot in each of the sidewalk boxes. And for the next minute, we focus on breathing. This is better than thinking about how big the hill is and how much more distance is left before the run is done. With all this said, there still is going to be a day here or there where other factors make the run even harder and walking occurs. The important thing is going back on another run later that week or soon after it.

Another example of resiliency and the winning mindset is no deficit is ever too large. What happens if you are down two touchdowns, and you give up another touchdown? In youth sports, the team that's losing typically slouches and moves slower because their mind tells them the game is over, and, in a couple minutes, that deficit becomes five or six touchdowns. Someone with a winning mindset doesn't like being down three touchdowns, but that athlete is doing everything in his or her power to get the deficit to two touchdowns and then to one because they know they can do it.

3. Work hard until you achieve your goal.

There's a saying that effort beats talent. One could be naturally gifted, but if they don't work hard at their craft, then they will eventually be left behind. In high school, or higher education, there are naturally gifted students that have Cs or Ds for grades. Just because they did well before does not mean they can just show up to class or just the exams. The students that come to class and pay attention, take good notes, and practice at home do much better.

Those with a winning mindset use these three p's: practice, preparation, and patience. There's a saying that practice makes perfect. Well, one can go through the motions at practice, or coaches can be glorified babysitters and just stand there during practice instead of having cultivated a culture of learning and hard work. Therefore, PERFECT practice makes perfect. As a coach and a player, you need to be patient. If a skill has not been mastered or a play is not run correctly, then you can pause practice and focus until it is done correctly. Scrapping a well-designed practice plan is common for coaches that are patient and know what is needed to achieve the larger goal.

Practice, preparation, and patience are important, but, putting in extra work might be the catalyst that brings it all together. Often while watching sports on tv, the announcers would talk about the hills that were run in the offseason to condition for the fourth quarter of a game, or the shots taken after a game in the gym because of a poor shooting night. Those with a winning mindset never get out worked.

4. Learn and grow.

There's a reason why teams watch film on past performances. Losing should be treated as a lesson, not a nail in the coffin. Losing should be treated as a report card of what needs to be improved. If you lose and do nothing after it, then odds are you willl lose again when presented with a similar situation. Granted, some sports losses happen despite you performing at your best, and no change would have resulted in a win.

As a coach, I always took pride in making adjustments. People would compare it to playing chess while the other team is playing checkers. This was especially necessary when our teams were outmatched via either skill, speed, size, or experience. Teams must learn and adapt during the offseason. They must look at what strengths and weaknesses they had in the previous season and grow from it. Teams must get better in season from week to week via practice. Teams with a winning and growth mindset get better at half time of their games. They refocus, and they perform better in the second half. Winning teams adjust between quarters. They take a step back and think about what worked and what did not. If there is a large deficit, teams with a winning mindset do not fret. They dig in. Teams with a winning mindset adjust after a play. Teams with a winning mindset do not take three or four plays to adjust. They do not take three or four minutes, or three or four quarters to adjust. They reset and make changes right away since they are always learning and growing.

Having a goal in mind must come first. But the other 3 keys can be in any order. Working hard, learning and growing, and being resilient are constants with a winning mindset. Those with a winning mindset exude confidence. The winning mindset is contagious. Having the winning mindset allows you to accomplish anything you put your mind to. Beating someone with a winning mindset is very arduous. Imagine facing a team or a coach that is notorious for coming back from any deficit. Do you feel confident with a four-score lead against them? What is the other team with a winning mindset thinking down 28-3? What are the players saying to each other on the sideline or on the field? What are the coaches saying if they have a winning mindset?

I was not there on the Patriots sideline, but when they were down 28-3 with less than 20 minutes remaining in the game, I knew they could come back. I imagine the players and coaches first reminded each other what the larger goal was. Someone probably mentioned that they did not come that far and prepare so much to give up and lose the Super Bowl. Next, instead of looking at the score and seeing an insurmountable four score deficit, I bet the players and coaches were doing the math and calculating what was needed by possession and by play. At this point, the Patriots had to show resiliency and play the hardest they had ever played while making tactical adjustments from their past mistakes. With their winning mindset, 28-3 became 28-9 with 2:06 remaining in the third quarter. Then 28-12. Then 28-20. Then 28-28 right before the end of regulation. The game ended with a 34-28 victory for the Patriots. A surprise to many, but not to those with a winning mindset.

Some of you are reading this because you want to have the winning mindset. To do so you'll need to learn what is the real secret to winning.

The great thing about having a winning mindset is you can use it with many things. Having a sports background and being a coach, I naturally think of sports or competition as a great place to have a winning mindset. Here are a couple other facets of life that could benefit from it:

Education	Nutrition
Professionally	Relationships
Health/Wellness	Financial well being

Take your winning mindset and put that energy towards something you desire. Be determined with your actions. Win the day. Win the week. Win the month. Win the year. Win!

ABOUT THE AUTHOR:

Social Media:
IG @hosstabrizi
FB @hoss.tabrizi
LinkedIn: @hosstabrizi
Email hoss.tabrizi@nm.com

Hoss Tabrizi is the son of Mehdi and Nahid and brother to Nahaleh. He's married to Carolyn, and together they have three children: Maximus, Mia, and Michael. He's a financial advisor, coach, bestselling author, public speaker, and community leader.

Hoss genuinely wants to help people become better and to discover their inner greatness. He cares about seeing improvement in himself and in those that he interacts with. Hoss communicates with people in a way that motivates them to have confidence and conviction on their journey towards self-improvement in their personal, professional, and financial lives. Just like his father, he wants to leave this world better than he found it.

DREAM, DARE, & DISCIPLINE
Kenneth Wilson

For me the winning mindset takes me back to my childhood. I was a huge sports fan. Once I learned how to play basketball, I did what most kids would do. I would go to the court or field and try to mimic the greats I saw on tv. I would imagine myself in the Super Bowl or the NBA Finals, making the last shot or final play to win the game. Every single time I would make the shot, or I wouldn't stop playing until I did. I would cheer, yell, and scream just like my heroes Michael Jordan, Magic Johnson, or Jerry Rice. I would spike the ball and pump my fist in celebration. In my mind I had just won the championship. I would really feel the joy and excitement, and sometimes cry tears of joy.

Even though I was a child those moments were the foundation of my winning mindset. I learned what it felt like to win. I learned what believing in myself was, and what it felt like to me. Every time I took the shot I believed it would go in. I never imagined a scenario where I missed the shot. I also watched and studied my sports heroes. I watched how they prepared, played, and celebrated when they won. I would later mimic their behaviors and movements to try to be just like them. I wanted to be a winner, before I really knew what that meant.

I carried that same mindset into adulthood. I had learned what a winner was and wanted to be one in everything I did. The mindset I carried as a child matured and evolved along the journey. I had also learned what losing felt like, and I did not like that feeling at all. I was very competitive and would take it personally. I always felt like I could do more. It did teach me to be humble and learn from my losses, which in turn made me a better person and competitor.

As I moved into business and entrepreneurship, I continued to carry that same winning mindset. For those who don't know, starting and operating a business is an extremely difficult undertaking. It can be life-altering and stressful. My experience as a first-time entrepreneur was no different. I knew I had a great idea, and some previous experience and expertise in my field. What I did not understand was that I had to change my mindset. I would often doubt myself and the business. At times I wasn't sure if I would succeed. I had lost the winning mindset that I developed as a kid and carried into my adulthood. That same winning mindset that helped me become successful in other areas of my life and early career. I didn't realize that the same winning mindset worked in the business world as it did in every other part of my life. Once I began to apply the winning mindset my business ventures began to flourish. I began to experience success and accomplish the goals I set.

Over the years I have learned some valuable lessons and practices that have guided me in my entrepreneurial journey and my life. These three basic principles that I practice are DREAM, DARE, AND DISCIPLINE.

DREAM

For me it always starts with a dream. Other people may use terms like vision or create. This is when you begin to visualize and see the path in front of you. This takes me back to the basketball court as a child when I could see myself taking the shot and winning the game. You should be able to visualize yourself in that situation.

You create the vision of what the outcome will be and believe that it will happen.

In entrepreneurship, the dream is the starting point. These are the initial thoughts and ideas of what you want. It may not be clear at first. It may start off fuzzy and abstract at first. Over time you will begin to develop a unique idea.

In our everyday lives dreaming is important. I'm not talking about dreaming while we sleep, but visualizing and goal setting. It is similar to the process described for entrepreneurship. Every day we have things to do and tasks to complete. We have short term goals, and long-term goals. We often have big ideas that come and go. They all start with some sort of vision of how things will go. We try to plan our days and plot our routes in advance. "Dreaming" or visualizing allows us to do that. Most of my days have been planned in advance. I have coordinated and planned the locations I need to attend. I have also visualized and planned the routes and methods of travel needed to get to the locations. However, there are some days when plans change. For example, a meeting may get cancelled in the last minute. Those changes can make me feel disorganized, and can throw my day completely off.

Dreaming will not give us all the answers. Dreaming is a starting point. It gives us a sense of initial direction or purpose. Our dreams and visions may change over time.

We must allow ourselves to be dreamers. We must continue to see our goals, and truly believe that we can achieve them. We must be able to experience our completed goals before we complete them.

Dreams are the foundation to having a winning mindset.

DARE

First, we dream, then we dare. We must have the courage and the drive to fulfill the dream. When I was a child, I would dream of taking the game winning shot. Then I had to go to the playground to physically shoot the basketball to take the game winning shot. That is the dare. It is not enough to dream. We must take the steps to act on that dream. I've always liked using the word dare to describe my actions. It defines the forward progress I need to make to accomplish my goals. It is about taking chances, or what some would call the leap of faith.

Entrepreneurship and being creative are very similar to me. You are creating a business or venture. You're daring to take a chance to create. You must take the dream and transform it into an understandable and realistic concept. This is where strategic planning, goal setting, and physical actions come together. You can't just sit around with the dream and hope it happens. You go make it happen. You cannot be afraid to act on your dreams. You may be afraid to fail, but you'll never know if you don't try. To dare you need motivation and determination from the dream. That will give you the fuel you need to keep going.

Back to my original example, the feeling of making the winning shot and winning the championship was my "fuel." That feeling of winning would motivate me to keep shooting the ball until I made the shot. I would keep shooting and practicing until I made one shot. I would dare myself to keep going. In my mind, winning was so fun and I wanted to keep doing it. It drove me to work harder to make the shot.

In entrepreneurship and life, the dare may not always be present. With the ups and downs sometimes, we lose our drive. It has happened to me at different times in my life. I have experienced burnout in my career. I've faced tough times. In those times I have been able to go back to my dreams and remember why I started. There have been times when I lost sight of the original dream, and I was on a completely different path. Other times I did the opposite and started with my drive and passion, but I had no vision of what I was supposed to be doing. In all those situations I found it best to take a step back and refocus. It may have been a difficult decision, but it needed to be done.

Dare is action. Dare to create. Dare to live.

DISCIPLINE

Discipline is very important to me. I would not be here today without being very disciplined in my life and career. I believe it is what separates entrepreneurs, athletes, and other people of high performance. Discipline is the rules, conduct, and boundaries we live by. It helps us stay focused and gives us the fortitude we need to stay on track.

To make the game winning shot I needed to learn how to shoot first. I had to watch and study my favorite players. In my life and entrepreneurial journey discipline keeps me on track. If dare is action, then discipline as the rulebook for how I play. It keeps me grounded as I navigate entrepreneurship and life.

Early in my entrepreneurial career, I often got frustrated by the lack of time I had to hang out with my friends. I was working a day job and trying to start my business during the night hours. My friends would beg me to take a break and come out. One time I decided to take a break and go out. At that time, I didn't have the discipline to know when to stop. One night became two, and two became three. Before I realized it, I had lost a lot of time (and money) hanging out. I was also behind on my goals and losing sight of my dreams. I had to learn how to find the balance and properly allocate my time to be productive, but also find some time to have fun.

Discipline is different for everyone. We must learn and figure out what rules and boundaries work best for us. Life experiences and studying other successful people may be a good place to begin.

We need discipline to guide us to a winning mindset.

My winning mindset may have begun during childhood, but it is a never-ending process. As dreams come and go, my dare and discipline guide me throughout my life. As an entrepreneur they have allowed me to create various ways to help people. In my personal life they guide me as a husband, father, friend, and member of my community. It's not always easy. Life and entrepreneurship have many challenges. Possessing a winning mindset can make the journey a little easier.

Continue to dream, dare to keep going, and have discipline to see it through!

ABOUT THE AUTHOR:

Social Media:

IG @mrkennethwilson

FB @mrkennethwilson

LinkedIn: @kennywilson65

Email kennywilson65@gmail.com

Kenneth Wilson is a native of Silver Spring, MD. He is the Founder and CEO of Men of Stature and Black Squirrel Media. He has professional experience in business, education, politics, and public safety. He is also a passionate community advocate who has worked with people globally.

As a consultant, he has worked with businesses, non-profit organizations, churches, and political outfits all over the world. He has developed programs that have helped dozens of aspiring entrepreneurs begin and pursue their business dreams.

He also has a passion to be a voice in the community, which includes hosting several podcasts and virtual shows. Kenneth can be heard weekly as Co-Host of the Community Coalition Show, Reason & Rhyme Podcast, and The Speakeasy Show.

As a public speaker, he discusses issues involving the Black community, with a focus on Black men. He also discusses and teaches seminars on business development. In the field of safety, he is a certified CPR/First Aid Instructor. He teaches courses in person and virtually.

Accomplishments
- 2016 President's Lifetime Achievement Award Winner
- Two-time Bestselling Author
- Founder and CEO of Black Squirrel Media & Men of Stature
- Creator of the B.LIT Festival & Black Squirrel Media Network
- International Safety Expert and Community Advocate

MENTAL HEALTH AND THE WINNING MINDSET
Kristen Davis

A Winning Mindset has so many necessary moving pieces that come together to make it a reality. To understand what an actual winning mindset consists of; it helps to break it down into its core. Winning can be defined as gaining through work or enduring. The mind can loosely be associated with the collective conscious of a human, the brain, or even the soul, depending on who is describing it. To be set, means to be fixed, made permanent, or ready. Therefore, having a winning mindset can be regarded as having your conscious mind permanently set to gain. In many cases that gain is a goal or a new situation. That mindset and desire to gain is usually attributed to a positive change in your life. You must train that mindset to be permanently fixed on the win.

As a licensed mental health therapist, mindset makes up a huge part of the work that I do. Experts in the field agree that mindset will shape the behaviors of the person. Whatever that mindset is, it will heavily affect outcomes for that person. Simply put, the more you fix your mind on something, the more likely you are to experience the desired outcome. If you fix your mind on succeeding, the behaviors needed for that success are likely to follow and success will be more likely. The more we think about things, the more likely we are to try to make those things a reality. In doing that, those behaviors exponentially increase the likelihood that success will happen. Of course, this is not full proof. There are always other things at play and circumstances outside of our control. However, focusing your mind on success, winning, and desired outcomes makes it very likely that good things will follow.

How does a person begin to put themselves in a mindset to win? I would argue that a big part of it is mental health related. Without sound mental health, success and winning occur, but may not be able to be maintained. We see this many times in media with rich and famous people having an abrupt "fall from grace." In these cases, luck may have played a larger part than having a winning mindset. In these situations, we can also see things like talent and hard work. All of this is needed for success as well. However, if you only have these pieces, without the mindset, it may still result in the inability to maintain the things you have worked so hard for. That is why it is important to also have a winning mindset. Of course, there should still be hard work, resilience, and talent. If that is coupled with the appropriate mindset, then the ability to get and maintain success is elevated. Sound mental health is extremely important to making sure this happens.

One thing that is important to mental health and the winning mindset is addressing things from the past that have not been worked through. It is always tempting to push away difficult emotions that come up based on things that have happened to us. This could be huge traumas, like a death or loss, or even unresolved issues with family or friends. Almost anything could be holding someone back from having that winning mindset. Unresolved issues will try to convince you that you cannot be successful and that you do not deserve the things you want. Past traumas and hurt can block out the idea that you can have a good life and win. That's why it is so important to address things that have hurt you and feelings that you don't like to bring up. When avoided, difficult emotions will always return, likely worse that when they first surfaced.

It may be difficult to start dealing with these feelings, but you need only to take one step at a time. First, acknowledge the emotions that are difficult to work through. Notice which emotions come up and get in the way of the winning mindset. What is stopping you? Once you've identified the emotion, it is important to stay in it. Instead of pushing back the emotions, try to experience what it feels like. By acknowledging the emotions that are difficult, you are giving them respect. By sitting with the emotions and respecting them, they lose power over you. You are better able to understand and live with the difficult feelings once they are acknowledged. These feelings do not necessarily go away, but acknowledgment is the first step to dealing with them.

After the difficult feelings are acknowledged, and you become comfortable with sitting with them, you can then look a bit deeper into the faulty messaging that the emotions are causing within you. Many times, when experiencing difficult emotions, they come with irrational thoughts and beliefs that can sabotage your success. Once you've identified and acknowledged these thought and beliefs you can begin the work of breaking that down. You can do this alone, or it can be done with a professional if it seems too difficult. How would you know if a feeling is irrational? That depends on the thought as well as the thinker. A quick way to identify it is to ask yourself if it really makes sense or is it a reaction to a specific event. For example, if you think "I will never be successful," you can ask yourself "does that make sense?", "why am I thinking this?", "Do I have proof that I will never be successful?" Irrational thoughts tend to overgeneralize and catastrophize an event. If you have one bad day or have one bad experience, you may think all experiences will be that way. If you didn't succeed in one thing, you may begin to start thinking that you will never succeed, but this is certainly not true.

Continue to try to sit in the difficult feelings. While doing this, remind yourself that the bad feelings are temporary. It is something that will surface or resurface depending on what is happening. With that knowledge, you can continue to talk yourself through the difficult feeling and remind yourself that it will pass. The more you do this, the better you become at living with feelings that may be difficult.

It is also important to take some time with past issues. One principle that is consistent in mental health is that of the Inner Child. Some people have past hurts that were never healed. Because of this, the bad feelings that come out and maladaptive thoughts may belong to the inner child whose feelings were never addressed. Many inner children never felt safe, or stable. They then become adults who do not believe they deserve these things. Another example of this can be someone who experienced bullying as a child. If never addressed, the inner child remains in a place of low self-esteem and fear. The adult may have issues with feeling worthy of success. They may also come to fear success or notoriety because of the past unaddressed feelings.

In addition to those questions, you can also begin to work to resolve the irrational beliefs and replace them with thoughts that align with a winning mindset. It can be a bit of a process when unlearning faulty beliefs that have governed your thinking for a very long time. You must exercise patience with yourself. It will not be something that transforms quickly. Positive behavior adjustments come from reframing your thoughts about what happened. The way that you begin to do that is associate better feelings with the event. This does not mean that you can make happy feelings go along with a traumatic event or loss. What it does mean is that you can try to reframe what happened to bring about a change in your emotional response. Instead of thinking about the unpleasant things that you experienced as something that happened to you, try to rephrase the event as something that empowered or taught you. Perhaps you learned resiliency, or experienced spiritual growth. This does not mean that you forget the things you have gone through, nor that they were not terrible. Reframing does not change what happened. It just gives you a different way to think about what happened. The goal is to minimize the unpleasant emotions that surface when you think about it.

Once you have acknowledged the irrational thoughts and unpleasant feelings that interrupt you, it is time to focus on retraining your thoughts to be in line with that winning mindset. This is important because a winning mindset will help shape the behaviors and thought processes associated with success. It will also help you achieve what you want in life. When discussing a winning mindset from a mental health perspective, your thought patterns are one of the most important things to keep in mind. Once you eliminate the faulty thinking patterns that were ingrained in past bad experiences, it is easier to begin building up thinking patterns that help push you towards more success. These thought patterns should be a conscious decision that is made every day. The best thing about developing these thought patterns is that they will belong completely to the person imagining them. Every person has a different thought process that inspires success.

When developing your own set of thought patterns, it is important to ask yourself what the goals you wish to achieve are. Then you can develop your new way of thinking. What is it that you want to happen? What do you want to accomplish? What type of life would you like to live? These questions will help you begin identifying the healthy thought patterns that you will incorporate into your life. If that goal is physical fitness, you should begin thinking about your fitness goal and how you will accomplish it. You can start with thinking about how often you will go to the gym, and the kinds of exercises you will do. It is also important to begin associating positive feelings with your goal setting and thinking. It is not enough to think of what you must do to be successful. You must be excited to take those steps. That can be accomplished by doing additional reframing. Instead of saying that you "have to" go to the gym, you can say that you "get to" go the gym, as if it's a trip. Start thinking of these things as a treat, or something that is step one in the awesome life that you see for yourself. Again, this will take time and practice, and it is important to not get discouraged. Set your thoughts with repetition. Repeating these thoughts, whether out loud or in your head will make sure that you begin to really ingrain them in your subconscious.

Another way to adopt positive thinking patterns and a winning mindset is to incorporate affirmations into your daily routine. Many people are afraid of affirmations or simply do not know where to start. It is actually simpler that what some may think. An affirmation is defined as affirming something, and even better, emotional support or encouragement. Staying with that definition, then, only requires you to use a phrase that encourages you. When broken down in that way, affirmations should be easier to come up with. You can also borrow affirmations from other people, like friends, a spiritual leader, or a therapist. It is completely okay to take some cues from others if the affirmations speak to you and your subconscious. It is important to make sure you interact with it daily. Interaction with affirmations, can mean reading it aloud or silently, thinking the positive thought, or listening to the affirmation on a video or recording. The way you interact with the affirmation is not important if it works for you. Those affirmations will begin to shift the way you think throughout the day and help you to keep a positive energy throughout.

Another important aspect of a winning mindset is self-care. I go through this concept regularly with clients to make sure that they understand how important self-care is. When you take time to exercise self-care, you demonstrate to the world, and yourself, that you are the priority. It is very important to having a winning mindset. When the term self-care is used, many people think of spending a lot of money, or time, or having to go have others cater to you. That can be a way of participating in self-care. However, that does not have to be the case. It can be anything you are doing to stop and care for yourself. Affirmations are an example of self-care, as is regular exercise, and eating well. These things may not cost a great deal of money but are some of the best things you can do to ensure you are mentally well. The healthier we are, the less stress we have, which in turn heavily affects your mental state.

The more you practice self-care, the more you signal to the world that you are important. Self-care increases feelings of wellness and stability as well. The other piece to this is that you are continuing to put yourself at optimum functioning levels. The increased feeling of wellness allows you to think more clearly and make better decisions. Often, we hear about people who are over worked or stressed, have not taken time off, or stopped to care for themselves properly. When in that state of mind, the decisions we make may not be the best for us. They may be the best decision to get through that difficult time, but it may result in unforeseen issues later. By stopping to engage in self-care, we put ourselves in a better position to make decisions. The better we feel, the better our decisions are. The psychology of self-care impacts all other areas of functioning and is imperative to putting yourself in a winning mindset.

When focusing on creating the Winning Mindset, managing your intake is also important. To go to a new level, you must monitor what you think about and what you put into your mind regularly. If you only watch or listen to things that focus on negativity or non-productivity, then it will also begin to take hold of your unconscious. Likewise, only watching or being in environments that focus on your goal may also cause some stress. Moderation is key to being balanced and able to produce what is needed to reach your goals. There should always be time to take a break, decompress and do something unrelated. In that same token, negativity cannot always be avoided. For example, we must be able to keep up with current events, although it is not always pleasant. It is also extremely important to spend a great deal of time focused on achieving your next goal. Again, balance is the key. If you find that you are not able to reach your goal effectively, consider monitoring what you are intaking and adjusting accordingly.

Overall, to achieve a winning mindset, you must focus on your mental health. First, you must make sure that you have addressed negative emotions and past hang ups. This will free you to begin pursuing that next level. Next, you should focus on taking care of yourself, which allows your mental health to be at its best. You must also take this time to monitor what you are taking in, making sure that most of the time is spent being productive and moving towards your goal, while making sure to take breaks to stay balanced. By doing these things, you increase your mental wellness and can use your winning mindset to achieve your goals.

ABOUT THE AUTHOR:

Social Media:
IG @kristendavislpc
FB @kristendavislpc
LinkedIn: @kristendavislpc
Email kristen.gtrc@gmail.com

Kristen Davis is a Licensed Professional Therapist with years of experience in private practice. During her time as a therapist, she has worked in the areas of substance abuse and addiction, trauma, depression, anxiety, life planning, Transition, Neurodivergent populations and Career Readiness. Additionally, Kristen works as a Regional Transition Program Specialist for the Gulf Coast Region of Texas Workforce Solutions - Vocational Rehabilitation Services, implementing programming for students with disabilities and providing feedback on effectiveness to Regional and State administration.

She has a personal tie to Trauma, PTSD, and Depression after her brother was murdered. Although it was a horrible experience, this has helped Kristen to expand her knowledge on grief and overcoming substantial mental stress and strain. This experience was so transformative, that it moved her to write a book detailing her battle with grief and how to utilize therapeutic practices in real life and speak to audiences.

Kristen has a Bachelor of Arts in Psychology and Master of Science in Mental Health/Rehabilitation from Mississippi State University.

I FOUND MY LIGHT WHEN YOU LEFT ME IN THE DARK

Monica Earl Washington

God and confidence are everything and most people don't have it! You need God and confidence to make things happen powerfully within your life. To build and establish a winning mindset, you will need to have a strong effective prayer life which includes fasting and meditation in a higher God. For me to stay in the winning mindset it starts with me trusting God who provides peace. He gives a strong understanding of one's rights and wrongs.

Some people will say that you need a plan. When I left my rural southern town of Clarksville, Tennessee, I did not have a plan or anyone that supported me. What I learned when I was growing up was not to have babies in my teenage years, not to get in trouble with the law that would shame the family or the family name, to get a job, and always stay in an active Christian led ministry.

College or trade school was never offered to me, nor was it a topic in any discussions during my child rearing years. Therefore, no plan was established for me to thrive or build on because I wasn't informed of an educational plan.

I knew I had a plan and a goal without knowing it was a plan or a goal. That plan and goal was to marry a man that could provide for his wife and family. The one thing I do remember seeing from my small southern town was all of the strong men where great providers to their wives and family. Many of the women where home makers (stay at home parents), domestic workers (housekeepers), and some women were educated women that had careers. The men were seen as the most respected and highest of providers. I learned that if a man could not provide or bring anything to the table if "he" had a liking for you or if "he" was the marrying kind of man", then "he" would need to be able to produce and provide. This is what I saw and most of the men were not educated. However, they owned and work in the fields after working long hours in factory plants to provide for their wives and families.

When I speak of producing and providing as a man, I mean spiritually, financially, and emotionally. Loving and caring for a woman to make a woman want to accept a man's hands in marriage. Most of the men were very active or leaders in the ministry and that was a plus from where I come from. There was also Ft. Campbell, Kentucky military base, where I was born. This opened doors for many good military men who desired wives.

My main goal was to avoid becoming a teenage mother. I was very frightened of becoming a teenage mother and being jobless. My final goal was to avoid becoming a "bitter, mean, and resentful woman" based on what my mother deposited into my life. I did not know what verbal abuse was, but I do remember that I did not want to make my children regret the day they were born. I was often told by my mother about the mistakes she made. She took her anger and frustration out on me for being born unto the unknown.

God's mercy and confidence, yes, I had to have it growing up under such anger of what was unknown to me. From the age of 18 to my current age of 57, I have always worked 2 or 3 jobs. I don't know any other way but to work, the one good thing I inherited from my mother and my grandparents was to go to work.

Working created the winning mindset for me. I feel that being jobless would have created inconsistency. It would have prevented me from reaching and establishing any plans or goals. Being jobless creates heavy frustration and many other negative emotional actions that leads to more frustrations. It builds up negative fences around your life and consequences with no way out. Working opened doors for me to build confidence.

When I had my first son in my 20's, James "Tank", I started to become responsible. It was no longer just me. I knew how to fend for myself before becoming a mother. It was easy for me to go to work, slide out to high end stores, shop for the best clubbing attire, party all night, and go to work. Somewhere along the way I would get rest then do it all over again, but I was a young whipper snapper. The beginning of this new chapter started on May 29, 1987, and again on October 17, 1993. with my youngest son Reginald.

Children will make you responsible. Children need clean and safe living quarters, food, clothing, and medical care. I had to make sure my sons were prepared to go to school. I also had to make other decisions to ensure my children's safety. This meant no more partying or clubs. I made the choice to change my environment. It was not easy being a single woman who loved to party with high end VIP status people.

My first son's father died of a massive heart attack in 1988 at the tender age of forty. This was extremely very hard for me since it was a very close death that I experienced within the first year of motherhood. I was thankful that Tank's father was prepared and ensured that our foundation was financially secured before his death. He left me without the worry of providing for my first son. That opened doors for me to walk with confidence into motherhood by the time my second son arrived. I had a great instructor that left an amazing example for me in my early twenties.

As I was trying to build a plan and keep a winning mindset, I lost the only father figure I knew on the day I gave birth to my oldest son. I was unable to return home because I had lost six pints of blood and was unable to travel from Gary, Indiana back home to Clarksville, Tennessee for the funeral. Sickness and death kept coming. In 1988 my grandmother had a stroke, and I was left with uncertainty because she was very inspirational in my young child rearing and adult years. In December of 1988, I lost my mother.

The domestic violence I endured from my mother had come to an end, or so I thought. I had so many damaging things that were deposited into me from my mother who I remember as bitter, resentful, and mean to me. I later learned that my mother had an affair with a married military man, while being married to my father who was away in the military. When my father returned home to my mother, she was 5 months pregnant with another man's child. That man abandoned my mother and never acknowledged my mother's pregnancy or her unborn child. I later learned that my father loved my mother dearly. That had to be very heart breaking for my father, to watch his wife love a man who did not respect her and use her as a complete disposal dumping ground.

I suffered greatly from my mother's outside affair. She was verbally and emotionally abusive. My mother was angry all the time when I was in or out of her presence. I was not sure what I was supposed to do. I never understood why I was singled out to be called out of my name and degraded on a regular basis.

I could feel the anger when I was in her presence. I have many images in my mind of spit flowing out of her mouth as she would shout horrible degrading names at me for simply being born. My mother was broken by someone else, and I suffered for it. She would beckon with her finger for me to come toward her with a demonic frown on her face. It was the harsh combing of my hair, washing my face, and dressing me as a child harshly. I could see the difference of how I was being treated verses my siblings. I have no memory of my mother ever hugging or kissing me on my cheek or forehead.

The one thing that my mother did not abuse with me was finances. She was extremely good to us, and I don't remember any hard times being raised by my mother. I never had to share anything with my sibling, not even a bedroom. My mother was a great protector. She did not have any people around us that did inappropriate things to us, and I am truly thankful for that. Appearance was everything to my mother, pleasing people was important to her. That may have played a major role in why I did not experience financial abuse from my mother.

My mother was a master of verbal abuse towards me. Even after her death, I continued to hear many things but the one thing that I remember was her saying, "I could spend a million dollars on you, and you will never be as pretty as your sister."

She would often say it loudly when family, her siblings, cousins, and her friends were around. They would all laugh. I just remember the laughter. I remember people laughing so hard until they would cry.

The only people that did not entertain my mother's verbal abuse were my grandmother and grandfather. My grandmother would be attacked verbally as she would come to my defense. My grandmother often would let my mother yell and scream then come back softly and say, "Emma Louise, you are out of order, and you are provoking this girl (Neecy) to wrath"

I had no real understanding what "wrath" was. I remember that I was always angry with my mother, wanted to hit her, someone, or something when my late mother would attack my grandmother verbally. I was used to being under her attack, but not my grandmother. If that is what "wrath" meant as a child in my mind, then my grandmother was correct, as I later learned.

I knew that my introduction to abuse from my mother was not normal. I remember that I played with the white Barbie and Ken doll set until I was about 17 years old. I had everything for my Barbie set, I had the dream house, the convertible car, and the handsome husband Ken. Back in the early 70's going into the early 80's if you had Barbie and all the trimmings you were considered spoiled.

I found beauty while living in the shadow of darkness of my mother's brokenness from a letter that was read to me a day after her death. This letter confirmed that my sibling and I did not share the same father, but my sibling shared my father's last name. This is where the confusion stopped for me.

I was 21 years of age and at that moment I felt it was cold-blooded, yet it was beginning to make sense. Later in February of 2020, it all made sense when I learned of the affair my sister and husband had. The clarity of the abuse was clear. It was clear that to me that the lies were hidden. It was clear that I was abused for something that was not my fault.

My own mother attempted to destroy and break me because she was broken into pieces. One thing that came to my mind when I began to write this chapter is a Waterford fine crystal water goblet. I chose the Waterford because I grew up on Waterford, which was a collection of my late mother and grandmother's. They collected it from a jewelry store in my hometown of Clarksville, Tennessee, called Joy's Jewelry, which was known for very high end fine diamond, rubies, pearls and crystal. In that small window, the owner would line up the finest and latest of the Waterford collection. My mother and grandmother would ride by on some Sundays after church to see if Joy Jewelry had a new Waterford collection in the window. I remember my mother and grandmother would pay about twenty to twenty-five dollars per goblet. They came in sets of six or eight, according to the collection. I remember one of the Waterford's goblets broke. It broke into very fine unrepairable pieces and there was no more use for it.

I was under pressure from my mother and I did not know it. I did not have a chance under her pressure as a child. I was tossed and driven in a tormented colliding tornado and hurricane of my mother's sin. Yet it was my grandmother's prayers that God kept my mind to find my own light. It was not until I saw Ms. Lucy's granddaughter's tattoo. I am not a tattoo person. I can't stand tattoos, but it was the script of the tattoo on Diamond that said, "I found my own light when you left me in the darkness."

My mother was the Waterford goblet, and she was broken into shattered pieces. I reminded her of love or hate for the sins she committed. For me I felt the hate all my life until I left my mother's home at 18 years old.

Diamond's tattoo script spoke volumes to me, I felt relieved in May of 2022 when I saw that script. I declared that I would not let my mother's darkness break me into pieces. I refuse to let the darkness of others put me in their narrow-minded boxes. I refuse to let the darkness of others define me though the many lies from jealousy, envy, and insecurities they wanted to place upon me. It was the script of a tattoo on Diamond that made me say "Hallelujah, I am not like my mother or my sibling, I made it out of the darkness by trusting God."

The most valuable thing that my grandmother could have ever deposited into me was getting me involved in church. We were up on Sunday morning getting ready for Sunday School and Sunday services. We attended services on Wednesday night. In the summertime I dreaded vacation bible school, but I went. Later in life I developed my own personal relationship with God. As my late grandmother Rosester Hoosier Johnson would say to me, "Tarry, you tarry Neecy and trust God. God will show up for you Neecy." Bigmama knew the hidden secret and her prayers prevailed it much for me.

The King James Bible that I study states in Proverbs 6:32, "He who commits adultery is an utter fool, for he destroys himself." Hebrews 13:4 states, "Give honor to marriage and remain faithful to one another in marriage. God will surely judge people who are immoral and those who commit adultery."

In February of 2020 I had to digest what my mother had done over fifty years prior. It would unfold later as a major factor in my life. When my mother became pregnant, it was wrong, and I was told not to address things with my mother, to let it go. But how do you do that when the signs of the generational curse are so close to trying to overtake your life. God was speaking for me to continue to "Tarry."

After the affair of my sibling and my now ex-husband, I understood the generational curse to be something that a person may practice and may believe it to be right. People can only walk together when in agreement of what is good, right, or wrong. Bonnie and Clyde believed what they were doing was right, and they both convinced each other what they did was right, yet they both brutally died. Pharaoh convinced an entire army that under his leadership it was right to keep people in bondage, yet Pharaoh and his army all died brutally as the Red Sea closed on them.

It made sense when my sibling and my ex-spouse had an affair. It was a curse on both sides. My ex-husband's father did it to his wife and died suddenly at a young age. My mother did it to my father and my mother died at the early age of forty-two. As a result, my sibling and my ex-spouse can walk together because they were in agreement from the generational curse.

I did not drop my mother's bondage in 1983, but I began to clean it up in 2020, it was too heavy for me to carry. I knew in February of 2020 I had to let go and let God fix it for me, because the generational curse was popping up too close in my life to attack me. Standing up in 2020 to the domestic violence as I watched my ex-spouse play victim. I knew the generational curse was too close to me and I did not want what Satan was directing unto to me.

Ignoring the verbal abuse had become a normal for me. I had this introduction at the age of five and it was normal for me, but this opened the door to physical abuse that leads to fear. Fear opens the door that can create a "Killer." I had to get out the broken person language. I began to see in 2020 that a broken person with the unhealed mentality will not produce a solid man or woman.

2nd King 4th Chapter

"I found my light when you left me in the darkness." I have learned that I was never one with envy or jealousy. No one can get to a winning mindset being stagnated or hating on others' blessings. I look at my winning mindset like the Shunammite widow woman who lost her husband who died leaving a debt. Later, the widow woman had a knock at the door from bondsmen that wanted the debt her husband left, or the bondsmen were coming to get her sons to place them in slavery. The widow woman said she had nothing but a little bit of oil, so she thought.

After realizing that I was not going to carry my mother's evil bondage upon me, I stood up to domestic violence in February of 2020 when the deadly COVID-19 virus hit. I was purposely left to die by turning off the lights in eighteen-degree weather, turning off the water, attacking my job with the intent to have me jobless, and plotting to have me incarcerated. All with the intent to have me grovel. It was then I began to take what little bit of oil I had, and I began to tarry all day and night, I began to move myself out of God's way. I stripped myself from all my fine clothing, minks, designer purses, fine gold, diamonds, rubies, and pearls. I detached myself from the half a million-dollar home that I received for my 2015 Valentine Days gift from my now ex-husband.

I paced a little while just as the widow woman did, but what the widow woman did not do was break down and cry, lose control or have pity for herself. It was clear to the widow woman that the bondsmen would be returning to collect money or her sons. The widow woman ran until she found the Prophet because she had an immediate emergency. The Prophet gave the widow woman specific instructions. The widow had just a little bit of oil that was not enough to fry two pieces of chicken. The Prophet told her to go collect jars of all sizes. In obedience, the widow woman did as she was instructed by God's Prophet. He told the widow to close the door behind her once she collected the jars and pour oil into all the jars until they were full. The more she poured the more oil came out.

I had to trust God in the mist of my betrayal, lies, deceit and darkness. I had no time to think about what the people were planning against me, because I was in an emergency. I had no room for panic to come in, God began to multiply the oil in my life just as God did for the widow woman. I told God I need major things:

1. I needed the lights and water back on that my Pharaoh was directed by my only sibling to turn off in eighteen-degree weather. My ex-spouse did everything he was directed with me having a disabled son in the home.

2. I needed the breaker back in the house that my Pharaoh was directed by my sibling and aunt's husband to remove out of the home in eighteen-degree weather to drive me out of the home.

3. I needed over sixty-thousand dollars for three different legal attorneys (domestic violence, criminal, and divorce). I learned about

the criminal charges created by my Pharaoh under the directions of my sibling, aunt's husband, his child, and family members.

4. I needed additional strength to work three jobs to meet all legal and other financial needs until my Red Sea Split for me. I was in bondage on purpose, and I kept walking towards the Red Sea.

5. I needed to remain in my half million-dollar home until the finalization of the divorce, as my Pharaoh had been removed by God where he settled into his own personal apartment eight minutes from the home we owned, with great comfort, and other adulterous affairs.

6. I needed the discipline to continue to pay tithes and offering.

I was not able to see how I was heading out of darkness into a winning mindset. I just kept myself out of God's way so God could continue to pour the oil in my life, and I could get out of demonic debt. I continued to tarry. God poured the oil in my life when eighty-five percent of the major income had left out of the home. I was not accustomed to paying no major bills; yet God came in and poured oil in my life. God turned all the utilities back on! God put the breaker back in the house! All attorneys were paid in full as of March of 2022! I worked all three jobs around the clock happily with great strength to continue until all legal debt was paid! I moved when I was ready! When God opened the doors for me to move, it was into my own independent beautiful spacious apartment, in the heart of DC by the nation's White House and the Capital! Once the finalization for the divorce was agreed upon, we sold the home! Within three weeks of moving into my new place on March 1, 2022, the home went on the market and remained on the market for five days.

The widow woman out of obedience followed what the Prophet instructed her to do. He told her to sell the oil to pay her debt and to live off the rest. God gave instructions to Moses to move forward to free the people. God kept his promise and spilt the Red Sea.

I kept moving and crossed over my Red Sea because I trusted God. I let go of everything because I knew I could not cross my Red

Sea with excess baggage, bondage or being in the wrong mindset. I had to release so I could get into the winning mindset. My winning mindset came in stronger once God revealed the true players in the satanic plan to destroy my life. Once God revealed everything unto me, God said for me to do nothing. I struggled with doing nothing, yet I trusted God because I did not want my Red Sea to close on me from being disobedient.

I made it out the darkness on God's divine guidance and strength! I made it out of the darkness by tarrying all night until forgiveness came in! I'm now free to live in a prosperous winning mindset! I have been delivered over people, places, and things! I had to get stronger to have my soul anchored in God, so I could tarry on for God to break the generational curses! I trust God to break the generational curse as I pray for family to maintain a winning mindset under God's direction!

ABOUT THE AUTHOR:

Social Media:

IG @monicaneecyearlwashington
FB @monicaneecyearlwashington
LinkedIn: @monicaneecyearlwashington
Email neecysoftandsweet@yahoo.com

Ms. Monica Earl Washington, nick name "Neecy," (short for Monica's middle name Denise) was born in Fort Campbell, Kentucky. She was raised in Clarksville, Tennessee, graduating from the legendary Burt Junior High School. She graduated from Northeast High School, Class of 1983. It is at Burt Junior High School where Monica found her passion for writing and learned to keep private dated and organized journals of her daily life.

Monica was the owner of Queenrodney Christian Cleaning Services of Jacksonville, Florida, cleaning million-dollar homes for elite clientele including several NFL football players. Monica is currently the owner of Neecy's Soft and Sweet Holistic Organic Southern Scents. Monica is the mother of two handsome sons, James "Tank" Earl, and Reginald Kilo Banks. She is the Gma of two beautiful angels, Corinthian "Corey" Earl, and Naomi Earl. Monica currently resides in Washington, DC and works for the Washington Headquarters (Pentagon). She loves to meet great people.

Monica famous saying, "Don't watch me, watch God!

AGAINST ALL ODDS
Reggie Rusk

A winning mindset begins in a person's subconscious mind before it's ever on display to the world. A person who has this strong unwavering belief that he or she will be successful no matter what obstacles are standing in their way. You must have a winning mindset to obtain success, or you will live your life building someone else's dreams. Show me a man with a positive perspective towards life, and I will show you a man that will have success. A positive mental attitude in my opinion is the #1 trait for a successful person. Even when things seem less than positive, a person with a winning mindset will always feel like there is a light at the end.

The beginning stages of having a winning mindset is first having a vision. If you can't see yourself having success, it's virtually impossible to obtain success. Envisioning yourself making plays on the field even before the game begins. Believing that you will have that house, car or business all begins in the mind.

I played in the NFL before I ever played one down. As a kid, I would envision playing for the Dallas cowboys. I watched football every Sunday religiously. As a kid, I knew almost all the players. Too Tall Jones, Tony Dorsett, Emerson Walls & Danny White. The legendary Tom Landry was the coach of the Cowboys back then. In high school, I used to see myself making plays before the game ever kicked off. Making that game winning play and helping my team win the game. I saw that last second drive to the basket to win the game a hundred times in my mind, finishing the race by a nose. The person with a winning mindset must have a vision of success.

The next trait a person with a winning mindset must possess is a strong commitment to the process. Your commitment level must be different than others. Sometimes this means long days and nights, no hanging with friends, and missing holidays with family. I remember missing many of my own birthday celebrations because of football practice. I would avoid going out with my friends all the time. I knew rest was more important the night before a game. I would always think about the most negative thing that could happen. That was my mental hack, this kept me out of trouble. I was committed to the entire process, and I realized there are no short cuts, just hard work, and tough life decisions.

As a young kid responsibility isn't something that is discussed. My younger adolescence came with the responsibility of watching over my disabled grandmother. I didn't understand at the time, but this was teaching me responsibility from the start. As I got older, responsibility became a huge part of my life. As a visionary, father and coach, I have to be responsible for other people. I have always been a selfless person, so being responsible has been very easy for me.

Nothing big in life happens if a person doesn't have some level of confidence in themselves. Confidence can sometimes be shaken in us, but a fundamental lack of confidence is a problem. Winning players have a level of confidence in their ability that others do not. They believe that they can accomplish anything.

Tom Brady is a prime example. He always thinks he can bring his team back in a game. His belief is, "Give me a shot, I'm going to lead us to victory."

There are thirty-one other starting QB's in the NFL and many do not have this level of belief. The pressure of doing the impossible often breaks a player's confidence. I can remember losing my starting job to Rhonde Barber in 1997. Coaches called me into their office and said, "We want to see what he can do."

I worked my ass off, my confidence was the highest it had been before this moment. I must say after that meeting my confidence took a turn. I didn't understand the business of the NFL, I took it personal. It hurt my feelings, lowered my confidence, and made me hate the game for a minute. As a player this will happen at some point. The key is to go back to your roots, your thoughts have to be on the positive things you bring to the table. In the NFL, you don't have time to have self-pity or doubt. There's always someone waiting on the sideline for you to slip up. My confidence eventually got back to the level it was before.

Everyone will have to deal with some type of adversity. If you're an athlete, adversity is a way of life. Athletes have to deal with adversity at least once or twice a season, whether it's an injury or losing your position. You must be able to overcome those setbacks. The key is to figure out why. If it's an injury, there isn't much you can do about that. If you lose your position figure out why your play is suffering. Usually, it's because of a lack of confidence. My advice is to have a meeting with your coach or boss. Your coach can let you know from his perspective, the issue he sees that you're having. Be open minded when listening to your coaches' thoughts. Take his criticism and apply it.

We must be able to persevere through adverse situations to grow. Perseverance is key to a winning mindset. Everything will not go the way you plan it, so stay focused on the goal no matter what.

I remember opening my second gym. The building was across the street from my first space. The space was located next door to a dollar store I used to frequent. I would walk by that space and envision it being my new location. One day I called the number to see the cost to lease this space. After speaking with the agent over the phone, I knew that the price was a little more than I could afford at that time. After looking through those windows for the next year, I decided to take a leap of faith. I called the agent again to ask for a tour of the space. I was determined to get this space! I had envisioned the paint color, the floors, and the design over a thousand times in my head before ever stepping one foot in the building.

After working out the deal, that new space became mine. I didn't let anything stop me from pursuing that goal of expanding my business.

It was 2001 when I realized my career had come to an end. The knee injury I suffered at age twenty-nine ended that chapter of my life. I had been playing football since I was eight years old. What would I do now? All I knew was football, practicing, locker rooms, being a football player. I was forced into an unfamiliar life with a one-year-old child. There would be no more meetings with the fellas.

This by far is the toughest transition in an athlete's life. We have been told where to be, what time to be there and our complete schedules for so long and now it's all over. You want to know what adversity really looks like; this is it. This isn't like a regular job that can be replaced.

I eventually got myself on track, started a business and applied the same mindset I had playing football. The same principles apply … mindset, vison, commitment, confidence, and perseverance. I turned that idea into a household name. Everyone loved bringing their young athletes to Coach Reggie and Next Level Sports. That's when I really figured out the trick to life. I had read books like *Think & Grow Rich* before, but I didn't quite get it. The reality struck me after starting my own business. I understood that if I want to accomplish anything in life, all I need to do is create a plan and execute it. It's literally that simple. I later took those same principles and created other businesses, become an author, NFLPA secretary, and mentor to my community. None of this happens without applying the principles as well as having a winning mindset. This past twenty-two years after playing football hasn't always been easy, I have had a lot of losses, but I will never give up on my dreams.

I hope that anyone reading this understands the power of the mind. You can literally accomplish anything you set your mind to, all it takes is a strong belief in yourself. Don't let anyone make you doubt your ability to achieve greatness. Surround yourself with others that think the same way. Like-minded people will keep you thriving for success.

Remember friends and family can be your biggest doubters. People are in two categories in my opinion ... engines or anchors. The engines are the people who empower you to become better. They're the people you learn from and are selfless when it comes to information or knowledge. The anchor, this is the person that weighs you down. They want to party when they know you should be in the bed sleep. They tend to not be happy for you after a promotion at work. Stay away from these people because they are not in your corner.

Last piece of advice, write down your goals. It's great that you have dreams and aspirations, but life gets in the way. I learned that writing my goals down in a location so I can see it daily works great. If you see it every day, you won't forget. Execution is the one thing that holds people back from achieving goals. Everyone has dreams, but only a few execute on those dreams.

ABOUT THE AUTHOR:

Social Media:

IG @coachreggie_
FB @coachreggie25
LinkedIn: @reggierusk
Email reggierusk@gmail.com

Beginning In 1996 Coach Reggie had the opportunity to play in the NFL for 5 seasons and played with 3 teams. Coach Reggie's path to the NFL was not a straight one.

Reggie knows first-hand how difficult it is for a young athlete. He had no offers after his senior year in high school and elected to take the junior college route to continue his education. Reggie's college coaches made a huge impact on him and his success. Growing up in a single parent household, those relationships were invaluable to Reggie's success. After two successful seasons, major D1 colleges were calling. Ultimately, he chose the University of Kentucky and played his final two collegiate seasons there.

Coach Reggie is a former student-athlete and graduate of the University of Kentucky. After watching numerous athletes lose opportunities due to failing grades, low SAT/ACT scores, and lack of recruiting awareness, His mission is to turn dreams into reality by helping student-athletes better prepare themselves physically, academically, and mentally. Play for success has aligned with many athletes, business owners, professionals in the community to create a realistic picture for students of every background.

ABOUT THE LEAD AUTHOR

Sugar Ray is a Motivational Speaker, Author and the CEO of Claim Your Destiny Enterprises, LLC! He has worked with several organizations across the nation to impact the lives of several thousand people! He speaks with organizations about overcoming obstacles in life, improving performance, increasing self-confidence and strategies for tapping into their full potential!

His company Claim Your Destiny Enterprises, LLC. focuses on research not theory. Sugar Ray Destin, Jr. is a nationally sought after motivational speaker. He empowers audiences with his message of hope, passion and the unlimited potential each of us possess! Sugar Ray empowers people across the nation with leadership programs, mentoring programs and college preparation conferences!

His publishing community, BOBM Publishing, LLC. had helped several people fulfill their dream of becoming published authors and create additional income streams using a proven system. To date, they have launched over 300 new authors to #1 Amazon Bestselling Author Status.

PICK UP THESE OTHER TITLES BY SUGAR RAY DESTIN, JR.

THE BUSINESS OF BOOKS

The Business of Books is a book designed to help authors become comfortable with the process of writing their first book. It will also take you into the world of marketing, branding and creating additional streams of income as an Authorpreneur.

CLAIM YOUR DESTINY!

Claim Your Destiny is the book that will help you tap into the unlimited potential you possess! If you are ready for your breakthrough this is the book for you! You will be empowered with the stories of average people who have achieved amazing victories! You will be introduced to tools that will help you master yourself and live your dreams! If you are ready, now is the time for you to Claim Your Destiny!

CLAIM YOUR DESTINY! (WORKBOOK)

The Claim Your Destiny Workbook is a perfect complement for the life-changing book! The workbook will take you through questions and activities that will force you to stretch as you tap into the unlimited potential you possess! Working through the workbook is like having the dynamic coaching of Sugar Ray available 24/7!

SUGARCOATED

This is a book of poems and affirmations about the inner and outer beauty of women. It is a celebration of the grace, elegance and phenomenal strength of the women in our lives.

To order your autographed copies visit
www.sugarraydestin.com/books-by-sugar-ray

www.ingramcontent.com/pod-product-compliance
Lightning Source LLC
Chambersburg PA
CBHW060253150626
46553CB00019BA/2110